BETH                    L
edited by Jennifer Underwood

# Our Help

four young children, two with cancer, one magnificent promise

*Our Help*

Copyright © 2014 by Beth Wetherell

All rights reserved. No portion of this book may be reproduced, stored in a retrieval system, or transmitted in any form or by any means—electronic, mechanical, photocopy, recording, scanning, or other—except for brief quotations in critical reviews or articles, without the prior written permission of the publisher.

Unless otherwise noted, Scripture is taken from the English Standard Version. © 2001 by Crossway Bibles, a division of Good News Publishers. All rights reserved.

All Scripture verses at the front of each chapter are in the ESV except chapters 3, 7, 13 (NIV). Scripture quotations marked NIV are taken from The Holy Bible, New International Version®, NIV® Copyright © 1973, 1978, 1984, 2011 by Biblica, Inc.® Used by permission. All rights reserved worldwide.

*For Brad, Matt, Elise, and Davis*
*– I love you*

*In memory of my parents, John and June Allen,
and my father-in-law, Warren Wetherell
Thank you for loving and serving our Savior
to the end. Your faith is now sight.*

# Contents

Chapter 1: Come and Hear ..................................... 1

Chapter 2: Our Help ............................................... 9

Chapter 3: Fear and Dread ..................................... 27

Chapter 4: Humble Yourselves ............................... 39

Chapter 5: Grace ..................................................... 51

Chapter 6: A Strong Tower ..................................... 59

Chapter 7: Wait in Hope ........................................ 65

Chapter 8: Fear Not, I Will .................................... 77

Chapter 9: Comfort in Affliction .......................... 89

Chapter 10: Take Refuge ........................................ 97

Chapter 11: Prayers of Many .................................. 107

Chapter 12: The One Who Helps ....................... 119

Chapter 13: Consolation ...................................... 129

Chapter 14: Your Faithfulness ............................. 141

Chapter 15: His Way............................................ 153

Chapter 16: The Best Help .................................. 161

Afterword............................................................. 170

*He whose life is one even and smooth path, will see but little of the glory of the Lord, for he has few occasions of self-emptying, and hence, but little fitness for being filled with the revelation of God. They who navigate little streams and shallow creeks, know but little of the God of tempests; but they who do business in great waters, these see his wonders in the deep. Among the huge Atlantic-waves of bereavement, poverty, temptation, and reproach, we learn the power of Jehovah, because we feel the littleness of man.*

— *Morning and Evening* by
Charles Haddon Spurgeon

## Chapter 1

# Come and Hear

*Come and hear, all you who fear God,
and I will tell what he has done for my soul.*
**Psalm 66:16**

Leukemia. This word grabs me every time I hear it, taking me to a place in my mind flooded with detailed memories, to a major event in my life. This is a story I often tell when I have the opportunity to share about my family, for it is a story that is uniquely mine, one I will never forget. The memories of it take me right back to that time, so much so, that every once in a while, during the month of September or October, the scent of the hospital returns. I can actually smell the memory. It doesn't matter how many years have gone by. When the night gets quiet and I'm alone with my thoughts, the leukemia story still has the power to invade my mind and emotions. It should. It is a significant, incredible story in the Wetherell family, and it has left its mark on my heart and life forever.

I was first introduced to cancer when my kind, gracious dad was diagnosed with lymphoma in 1991. He died six months later, stripping my mom, June, of retirement years with her dear husband and causing great sadness and heartache for all who loved him. He was 62. I was 30. This was my first, close-up view of cancer. I hated it, and I had a new awareness: anyone, any family member or friend, could get cancer. No one was exempt. I pushed that fear out of my mind by convincing myself that if this ever happened again, it would most likely be an old, distant relative who had lived a good, long life. It certainly would not be anyone as close to me as my dad.

In the spring of 1994, three years after my dad's death, I experienced some panic attacks and desperate thoughts that something terrible was about to happen. I didn't know why. There was nothing going on, nothing even simmering. Wes and I were in a solid, happy marriage. I was thrilled to be the mom of four beautiful little kids. We were very busy, yet Wes and I enjoyed the crazy life of parenting Bradley, 6, Matthew, 4, our little girl, Elise, 2, and our youngest, Davis, 7 months. I assumed my anxiety stemmed from the everyday stresses of motherhood, which had been even greater lately with all four kids getting the chicken pox. Elise got the nasty virus first, and Bradley, Matthew, and Davis came down with it exactly two weeks later. It had been a tough spring.

Another odd thing happened around the same time: Don Baddorf, a friend of ours, stopped me in church and asked if he could speak to me privately. He told me that while praying that week he had received a word from the Lord for me. Immediately he had my attention; this had not happened to me before. I don't remember the conversation word for word, but basically God had directed Don to tell me He saw and knew what I was going through, but I shouldn't worry because He was with me and would give me strength. I wasn't quite sure how to respond, but I felt God was simply sending me a very special word of encouragement as a mom. Admittedly, I was at times overwhelmed with motherhood, yet I really loved it. I'd wanted to be a mom my whole life. I thanked Don and tucked this reassuring God-moment in my heart. Don's words reminded me of the Scripture that says God gently leads those who have young ones, and I felt blessed to hear those words specifically to me as a mom. Looking back, though, I have a different perspective. I believe this was a prophetic, protective promise to me. God's amazing, sovereign rule over my life often leaves me breathless.

Through the summer of '94, our baby, Davis, constantly fought colds or ear infections. He became less active, and his naps grew longer. At first this seemed like

*Our Help*

a plus for me—any mom would love to have a good, solid napper, especially when she has three other little ones needing constant attention. But this perk soon became a concern when Davis started taking morning naps long after he had given them up. I was also growing worried about Davis' skin coloring. Susan Shelley, a friend from church who cared for Davis in the nursery one Sunday, commented on his skin tone when I picked him up. "His coloring doesn't look right, Beth. Have you had him checked by the doctor?" I had, twice, specifically to talk about Davis' pallor. The doctor wasn't alarmed—he had seen it before. Davis loved to eat sweet potatoes, squash, and carrots, and the depth of orange color from these yummy vegetables was now showing up through his skin. At least we thought this was the reason. Yet within a few weeks, even Davis' favorite foods were hard to get down. He didn't seem hungry. Was he too distracted by all the sibling activity around him? Davis was turning into a very quiet, complacent baby compared to my other three kids.

Warren Bradley, the first child to create the Wetherell family, was an incredible young boy (I know, all moms say that—but it was true). He was our only blond-haired, blue-eyed child. Inquisitive Bradley asked 1,000 questions a day and absorbed the knowledge quickly. His first, full, and most frequent sentence at age one was, "What's that?" Kindergarten at Ben Franklin

Elementary had been a great experience, and Bradley could hardly wait to start up again as a full-time student. I enjoyed watching him explore and discover new things. The excitement on his face was priceless. With all the great things to learn in first grade, I knew Bradley would bloom significantly this year. He had a compassionate, sensitive spirit for a six-year-old. He loved to listen to Bible stories and learn about Jesus. He was sincerely growing in his Christian faith. Bradley was also quite creative, active, and funny—oh, how he loved a good joke. He was a lot like my dad.

Matthew was double energy from day one and had determination with a capital D. He was unstoppable. I'd dropped to my knees more than once to ask God for wisdom to care for this little ball of energy. Yet he was sweet and sensitive, too, with the cutest smile that showed off a single dimple on the side. Matthew just loved to move, and, with great encouragement from his older brother, he took some hard knocks. But he didn't seem to mind. The harder he got hit, the better. When our city opened a new pool that summer, we signed our family up and went many times each week. Matthew would find a favorite spot to jump, cannonball-style, into the pool and do this same, simple trick again and again. He owned that edge of the pool for hours. So much energy, so much stamina, and I was so worn out by the end of the day with these two boys!

*Our Help*

At the end of August, I noticed a slight change in Matthew's face. I couldn't explain what it was, but something didn't seem right to me. I noticed it for the first time in a photo—a photo meant to capture Bradley on his new bike, but it captured much more. Matthew's face looked different, "bad" different. Maybe the nice summer tan was fading or maybe he was growing. I couldn't put my finger on it, but I felt immediate unease whenever I looked at that picture.

I also noticed a change in Matthew's energy level. Bradley had five friends over for a sleepover at the end of the summer. Normally Matthew would have been right there acting crazy with all of them. Not this time. I went downstairs to quiet the wild boys and hint about bedtime and then noticed Matthew, fast asleep in the midst of the chaos. That was strange. Matthew never missed a good party. A week or so after the sleepover, Matthew fell asleep during the day while he and a friend were watching TV. "That's really odd," I thought. I tried to come up with an answer as to why he was so tired. He didn't act or appear sick. I assumed he was having a little growth spurt.

His tough-guy character was also changing. I bought Matthew a new pair of gym shoes because he complained his others hurt him. We bought black ones—very cool—and Matthew was thrilled, until I started putting them on him. He winced and told me to stop hurting him. What was going on? I was putting his shoes on like I always did. After a few days of this problem, I put the cool shoes away and tried another pair. They were better, but I still had to be very careful holding his foot while putting the shoe on. All these odd, unexplained moments were unsettling, but they got lost in the busyness of our family.

One late summer day while rushing to get everyone in the car, I noticed Matthew was still riding his bike up and down the sidewalk. I told him to quickly put his bike away and get in the car. As he was turning onto our driveway, he fell in the grass. I was a bit annoyed because I thought he had wiped out on purpose. He was holding us up. As I finished putting Elise in her car seat, I heard Matthew start to cry. I walked over a bit frustrated with him for creating more of a fuss than necessary (this was normally the kid who played hard and liked it), but when I got closer and looked at his face, I immediately realized his pain was real. There was fear in his little brown eyes. I was taken back at his inability to get up and walk to the car. I assessed the situation as best I could. No broken bones, not even broken skin, so I helped him up, wiped away his tears, and away we went. Within the hour he recovered; yet from that point on he had a slight limp to his gait that affected his activity level. Matthew's two-year-old sister was becoming quicker and more energetic than he.

*Our Help*

Elisabeth Hope was our third baby and only girl. How fun it was to have pink clothing in the drawers and little dresses with matching tiny shoes in the closet. I have always loved the word "Hope" and was grateful to have a girl so we could use that name. It also had family meaning because Elise's great "Gammy" was Ruth Hope Straub, and she had a special place in all our hearts. Elise definitely had a mind of her own and could stand up for herself, even as a two-year-old. She was dainty and feminine yet tough enough to keep up with her brothers. Elise loved to imagine and pretend—something she enjoyed doing for years to come. At age two, she constantly played "mommy and baby" with any two objects she had in front of her: two stuffed animals, salt and pepper shakers, even a fork and spoon. If she didn't have anything on hand, no worries, she could play this imaginary game with her big toe and little toe! This daily exchange between objects was something unique about our petite Elise when she was two, and I found it so endearing. Mommy and baby, just like us.

## Chapter 2

# Our Help

*Our help is in the name of the* LORD,
*who made heaven and earth.*
**Psalm 124:8**

In September, Wes and I made plans to go away for a couple nights for our anniversary. Since Davis' birth the previous October, we'd had very few moments together, so we were intentional about setting aside a day or two around our anniversary for just us. I was a bit overwhelmed with "kiddy-land" at the Wetherell house and couldn't wait for this little getaway. On Thursday, September 22, the day before our special weekend, I ran into a problem. Davis was getting another ear infection, and this one seemed more serious than the others he'd had in the summer. He was running a low-grade fever, and when he was awake, he seemed irritated yet very quiet. I scheduled another doctor's appointment for that afternoon and then took Matthew, Elise, and Davis with me on a quick grocery run. If Davis was able to get some antibiotics in him and *if* he was doing better by the next day, Wes and I would still be able to go away for our anniversary.

While packing my bags at the Aldi grocery store, I glanced at Davis, who was sitting in the front baby seat of the cart. What I saw will haunt me forever. He had this blank stare on his face; his body slumped; and he looked so sad. Quickly I corrected my thinking: "No, not sad. Davis looks very sick." A horrible feeling shot through my whole body. Something was seriously wrong with my baby, more than just an ear infection. I wish even now this little guy could have told me what he felt, how terribly weak he was, how hard his little heart was pounding, and how painful every move was for him. I had no idea that my little baby boy sitting in that grocery cart was closer to dying than living.

On the way home I stopped by my mom's townhouse and shared my concerns. Davis tried to crawl around Mom's floor to keep up with Matthew and Elise, but as he began to follow them, he winced. "It looks like it hurts him to crawl," Mom said. I agreed and picked him up. My mind was racing. I was thankful we had a doctor's appointment for later that day. I wanted to go immediately, but Davis fell asleep again, so I waited. While he slept, I wrote down Davis' medical concerns

*Our Help*

and symptoms so I could go over each one, in detail, with the doctor. I needed answers.

Taking young children to the doctor is never a small task. I was grateful Bradley had been invited over to his friend Cooper's house after school, so I just had the other three. Once I was in the tiny exam room with all my kids, I shared every concern with Dr. Betti, emphasizing the increased sleep habits, decreased appetite, skin coloring, and the pain he had as he moved around. And now the ear infection was back; none of the previous antibiotics prescribed could clear this ongoing infection. Dr. Betti began examining Davis very carefully. He pressed down on Davis' abdomen—Dr. Betti's face changed. That bothered me. His countenance turned very serious, and I could tell he was alarmed by something. He drew blood for a CBC (Complete Blood Count) and asked us to wait a few more minutes for the results. By now Matthew and Elise had reached their tolerance level in the confined examining room, and I also needed to get Bradley from his friend's house. I called Wes to let him know I was running behind and asked if he could pick Bradley up on his way home from work. I told him the doctor was running some tests on Davis.

I waited and waited. Davis remained lethargic as I held him in my arms. I was glad I was going to get some answers. Finally, Dr. Betti came out of his office and escorted me to the waiting room, empty now, since the office had closed for the day. He asked that I sit down. Davis was on my lap. "Mrs. Wetherell, I think Davis might have leukemia . . ." He said this slowly, looking at me to see how I was taking this news. "Now it could be a blood infection, but with all the other symptoms, it's more likely to be leukemia. I'd love to be wrong about this, but you need to have further tests done. Davis is a very sick little baby. He is dangerously anemic; his white blood cells are extremely high; and his liver is swollen. I've already made a call to Loyola Hospital and have talked with their pediatric oncologist. He wants you to come over as soon as possible. Go in through the emergency room. I advise you to get there within a few hours."

That's exactly what Dr. Betti said. I remember it word for word, and yet I didn't get it—anemia, white blood cells, oncologist, Loyola . . . Numb and in shock, I whispered a strange thought that passed through my mind. "Wes and I planned a weekend away . . ." My voice trailed off. I don't know why I said that. Those thoughts, at that time, seem so stupid and selfish. Was I desperately trying to hold onto any sense of the "normal" life that was quickly slipping through my fingers? This pivotal point in our family story came without invitation, without planning or preparation. It caught me completely off guard. That's what cancer does. In a heartbeat, everything looks different. Everything *is* different.

We were on one path with our family and then, in a flash, on another, an unknown, terrifying one I didn't want to be on.

Dr. Betti, realizing nothing had sunk in, kindly repeated the information and gently replied to my random comment. "Could you cancel your plans?" he asked. Within a few seconds, reality set in, and this time the wave of information hit me right in the gut. Leukemia—oh no, that's cancer. CANCER! My eleven-month-old baby? Babies don't get cancer. A flashback of my dear dad invaded my mind. It was an awful memory. No way, not baby Davis.

Pam, the nurse, gently put her arm around me and led the kids and me out to the car. She buckled the kids in their car seats and spoke some encouraging words about childhood leukemia. It all sounded so strange and unfamiliar. The words were foreign. Was she talking to me? I had never had a conversation about leukemia before in my life.

Matthew's eyes were on me as I backed the car out of the doctor's parking lot. I tried my best to stay calm and focused. I didn't want the kids, especially Matthew, sitting next to me in the front passenger seat, to notice my fear. I would have expected Matthew to change the subject, saying something like, "What's for dinner?" or "I like the lollipop I got from Dr. Betti." But instead he asked, "What's wrong, Mommy?"

*Our Help*

"Mommy just got some sad news, Matthew." That was all I felt like saying. It was important to keep it short and simple. What else do you say to a four-year-old regarding the subject of cancer? Yet the next words that came from his mouth carried a completely different weight. They were profound, beautiful words that would become our family's anchor and hope through this entire journey. They were words with a promise, words sent from heaven above.

"Mommy," Matthew clearly said, **"Our help is in the name of the LORD, who made heaven and earth."**

Matthew had recently memorized Psalm 124:8 in a wonderful church program called AWANA. At that critical, desperate moment, God spoke. The Almighty God, maker of heaven and earth, the eternal and true One, used the tongue of a four-year-old child, my young son, to reveal His character and promise to me. What a faithful God. What a divine declaration. What a profound promise. In time I would begin to grasp the powerful significance of this verse, but not now. All my mind could think about was that our baby had cancer and I needed to get home.

Wes was still not home when I pulled in the driveway. This was before cell phones, so I had no choice but to wait till he and Bradley arrived to tell him the awful news. I somehow responded to the normal demands of feeding the kids; they were hungry and unaware that family life as they knew it had just shifted significantly. I put Davis in his highchair, though inside I was screaming that I shouldn't be making dinner right then. But what else could I do until Wes got home? I called my mom as I fed Davis. She was on her way over immediately. I called our pastor and his wife, Jeff and Lora Helton, dear friends of ours. Jeff arrived within minutes. He even beat Wes home. Jeff met Wes in the driveway and gave him a hint that tough news was on the way. Wes quickly got in the house. His eyes raced around the dining room and then met mine. Holding Davis in my arms, I told Wes everything the doctor had said. I could tell the news was barely sinking in. It's too much to comprehend when you hear it the first time. With little eyes watching us, Wes had to be careful how he responded. We didn't want to cause any more fear—they were already sensing so much—so we stoically talked through details with my mom, gave the three kids a kiss, and left with Davis for the emergency room at Loyola Medical Hospital in Maywood, Illinois.

We had no idea where we were going. Even now, whenever we head down Roosevelt Road toward Maywood and get to First Avenue where the hospital is, I always think of that horrible night and how we accidentally drove up to a small corporate building, thinking it was the hospital. Loyola Hospital is really, really big, a campus, but somehow we missed it. Wes and I look back

*Our Help*

now and chuckle about getting lost, but I didn't find it at all funny that night. Finally we found the hospital and then its emergency room entrance. When I walked in with Davis wrapped in my arms, a nurse immediately approached us. "We've been expecting you," she said. "We have a room all ready for you."

My heart dropped. I had still held onto the hope that Davis had a simple infection, but that faded as I watched how quickly the doctors and nurses took over and examined him. When they turned his little eleven-month-old body over and exposed his back to a very bright light, I gasped. I had never before noticed the multiple pinpoint bruises up and down his spine. (I later found out this symptom is called petechiae.) What was that? Did the doctors suspect child abuse? My head started spinning, and I felt sick to my stomach. The doctors and nurses were so concerned, but they weren't giving me a clue as to why. They did another blood draw on Davis and said they would be back with the results soon. It was not soon. We waited a long time, long enough to worry, to wonder, and then to hope and anticipate good news. I called my sister, Ruth. She, too, expressed the hope that it was all just a big mistake. *It's not going to be leukemia*, I told myself. *Everything's going to be fine.*

The results finally came back. An emergency room doctor told us the news. "Mr. and Mrs. Wetherell, Davis has a very high white blood count—over 180,000.

A normal WBC for a healthy person is around 5,000 to 10,000. We believe those white blood cells are not normal but leukemic cells. A bone marrow aspiration will confirm the diagnosis, but for tonight we need to get Davis admitted to the pediatric ICU (PICU). He is severely anemic and could go into cardiac arrest at any time. We will immediately start treating him with steroids to help bring the white blood count down. He will also receive platelets and multiple blood transfusions for his anemia."

We headed up to the pediatric floor. I was in a wheelchair with Davis in my arms. Wes was by my side. As we were wheeled through the hallway, Jeff and our friend Gail Salvatori joined us. My sad eyes gave them the confirming news. No one spoke a word as we headed to the floor that would soon become our home away from home.

In the PICU, the nurses took Davis from me and calmly told us they would need an hour with him without us in the room. It was an awful feeling to hand my very sick baby over to strangers in a really scary part of the hospital. But they knew we were not prepared to see them insert an IV into his tiny arm. We were not prepared to watch our baby become a cancer patient.

As the night went on, my brother Dave and a few more friends arrived. Their company helped pass the time, but their presence also emphasized how very sick

*Our Help*

Davis must be. They asked about his condition, but we had no answers. The nurses and attending doctors didn't have time to tell us anything because they were too busy caring for Davis; this had to mean Davis was in serious danger. That understanding made my gut twist with panic. I just wanted to be with him. Even as I sat with these wonderful, comforting people, my mind was screaming, "What's going on with my baby?"

Our family and friends left around midnight. Throughout the rest of the night, Wes and I spent as much time with Davis as we could, but the room was not set up for us to be in there, hovering over him. There was only space for a nurse, Davis in his hospital crib, and all the machines and monitors. The medical staff was also very strict about the amount of time we could spend with Davis. I was grateful I could see him through the window pane in the wall. Davis looked so small in the hospital crib and now so different. He looked deathly ill—the gut feeling I'd had in the grocery store was right. Why didn't I see this more clearly over the summer? Why didn't I get him to the hospital sooner? Did my slow response put him in grave danger? I was terrified. I felt I had not protected my baby. I felt like a horrible mother.

Davis finally fell asleep, and we eventually retreated down the hall. The nurses directed us to a small waiting room they called the family crisis room. *This is not a happy place*, I thought. I was so exhausted, I felt numb. I stretched out on the couch and tried to sleep. Around four, just before I finally drifted off, I remembered what little Matthew had said to me in the car earlier that afternoon.

***"Our help is in the name of the LORD, who made heaven and earth."***

I told Wes what Matthew had said, how he'd quoted the verse. I wondered what Psalm it was. I wondered what this meant for Davis. I finally, slowly fell asleep. Wes continued to check on Davis throughout those early hours of the day, and we were both up for good by six. We were meeting the pediatric oncologist for the first time.

Dr. Ammar Hayani, a young man about our age, walked in and introduced himself. I shook his hand and searched his eyes for assurance that everything was going to be all right, but his voice was quiet, almost solemn, his words were calculated, and I didn't want to hear what he said. He told us Davis had a type of leukemia called Acute Lymphoblastic Leukemia (ALL) and that infants were harder to treat. He said, "Thirty to forty percent chance of survival." *Please don't talk in percentages*, I thought. His message was short and to the point, and we didn't know what to say, what to ask, or even how to react at this point. He headed out as quickly as he had come in. Wes and I just sat in silence as he left

*Our Help*

the room. My first impression of Dr. Hayani was that he was cold and insensitive. I didn't like what he had to say to us, and therefore I wasn't too fond of him either. I had no idea we would so deeply appreciate this amazing doctor as time went on.

Davis responded well to the prednisone and transfusions and within two days was able to move to a regular room on the pediatric floor. He started to look and feel better—we were delighted to see him playing with toys in his hospital crib. He had his energy back and a rosy color flushed his cheeks. We felt like the worst was over. Wouldn't it be great if that's all it took for our baby to be healthy? We needed time for the seriousness of Davis' disease to sink in.

Leukemia is the most common cancer found in children, and ALL is the most common form of childhood leukemia. It is a disease that affects the lymphocytes, a type of white blood cell, which under normal conditions make antibodies and protect the body against infection. In ALL, these lymphocytes are not allowed to mature, and the normal mechanism for keeping their growth under control does not work. As a result, the growth of these immature white blood cells (called lymphoblasts or "blasts") is uncontrolled and disorderly, allowing them to accumulate in large numbers. As these leukemic cells, or "blasts," multiply in the bone marrow (the spongy material within the bones where blood cells are manufactured), other normal blood cells (red cells, platelets, and white cells) do not have enough room for growth, and the child eventually develops anemia (a decrease in red blood cells), thrombocytopenia (a decrease in platelets), and neutropenia (a decrease in white blood cells). Pallor and fatigue are caused by the anemia (no wonder Davis was sleeping so much). Bruising, nose bleeds, and petechiae (what Davis had all over his back) are caused by the decrease in platelets. A fever and other signs of infection are caused by the decrease in healthy white blood cells. Bone and joint pain may be present if leukemic cells invade bones or joints. Left untreated, these blasts push out the healthy cells, and the child succumbs to the disease.

The goal of treatment is the destruction of leukemia blast cells on the theory that this will allow for regrowth of normal cells. The treatment protocol consists of three phases: induction, which is the initial attempt to get the disease in remission; consolidation or intensification, aimed at further reduction of the leukemia cell involvement; and, lastly, the maintenance phase, a crucial phase in which remaining leukemic cells are eliminated or suppressed enough for the child's own immune system to overcome them permanently. This phase lasts up to two or three years without interruption. A relapse is when the cancer returns during treatment or after treatment has been completed.

*Our Help*

The doctors and nurses were unloading a great deal of medical information about leukemia to Wes and me those first few days. All of it was related to the care of our baby, yet the information wasn't easy to digest, especially when sleep deprived and emotionally drained. There was only so much we could absorb. Thankfully, our support was strong, incredibly strong. Friends and family poured into the hospital the first full day and continued to over the next nine days. Some just sat in the waiting room and prayed—we never even saw them, but they were there supporting us as we cared for Davis in the hospital room. Since my brother Paul was a pastor, he was allowed to visit any time of the day or night. I appreciated his pastoral and brotherly care. It was also comforting to hear that his church was praying for us. And our church, Glen Ellyn Bible Church, was also fervently praying for Davis.

I was overwhelmed with gratitude for all this prayer. The best antidote for my fearful heart was knowing there were hundreds of voices crying out to God, our Help, to heal our baby. I especially loved the huge banner made by the children from our church. We hung it up across one long wall in Davis' hospital room. We felt deeply loved every time we looked at it.

Back home, it was getting harder and harder to work out all the logistics for the other three kids, but our support in this area was also very strong. Two incredible

*Our Help*

women in our church volunteered to lead a huge team of people who stepped up to help. These co-angels were Jan Miller and Lisa Gaylord. Assisting them consistently was another church friend, Janille Eggert. They thought through many details regarding our three kids at home. Once they became aware of a practical need, they recruited a volunteer who stood ready to help. What a gift! These women not only coordinated all the volunteers, they personally took on the responsibility of caring for the needs of my family. They were my safety net for many months. Their endless acts of kindness included baking birthday cakes for my kids, providing backup meals and groceries when a volunteer couldn't follow through on her commitment, wrapping *our* Christmas gifts, and managing many day-to-day details in the Wetherell family. These dear ladies had their own young children and their own family challenges to face, yet they generously and graciously gave of their time to care for my kids. Their crowns in heaven will be far greater, far heavier than mine. I still marvel at their sacrificial love. I'm humbled to this day when I think about all they did for my family and me. I thank God for Jan and Lisa. I thank God for Janille and all the volunteers at Glen Ellyn Bible Church who faithfully cared for us. I thank God for the body of Christ. I couldn't have gone through this journey without their help.

*Our Help*

Even with this wonderful help, my dear, healthy children were feeling the effects of all the upheaval in our family. Everything was happening so fast. Bradley, Matthew, and Elise knew something was wrong, but Mom and Dad were rarely around to console them. They were being moved from one house to another, often separated from their siblings, and this caused anxiety for each of them. On top of that, Matthew wasn't feeling well. It was hard for this little guy to be without his mom or dad when he felt sick. We soon realized we would have to think through a better childcare plan, but for right now, we needed to focus on Davis at the hospital.

Davis began chemotherapy two days after diagnosis. On day four, a central line was surgically placed in his upper right chest. I hated the central line at first. It looked freaky, and I got upset every time I saw the tube hanging out of his body, but I eventually understood the importance and benefits of his having it. The line had direct access to one of his main arteries, so Davis never felt the pain of a shot (the kids called it a "poke") or a blood draw—which seemed to be taken every ten minutes in the hospital. Wes and I had to learn how to clean the central line site, replace the Tegaderm bandage at its point of entry, and flush the line with a saline or heparin solution. This cleaning routine had to be done daily at the hospital and regularly when home. Davis wore a tight, meshed tank to protect him from pulling his own line out of his chest (he was curious with his newly attached equipment and at times tried to play with it or tug at it).

Time seems to stop when you're in the hospital, and Davis' initial ten-day stay felt like an eternity. Wes and I wanted the other children to always have one of us home at night, so we took turns sleeping at the hospital. I was surprised there were no beds in the pediatric rooms at Loyola. We either slept on an uncomfortable reclining chair or the hard tile floor. Nights in the hospital were long, with constant interruptions, and the weight of Davis' condition pressed even heavier during the long, lonely hours. I was grateful when my friend Lora offered to stay with me one night. After Davis fell asleep, we crawled into our sleeping bags on the hard, cold floor, talked some, and then tried our best to sleep. Neither of us got much rest that night, but I felt so blessed to have a friend who was willing to share my discomfort and sorrow.

I also appreciated the nights I was home, in my own bed and with my other sweet kids. It felt so good, until I'd awake in the middle of the night and ache to be with Davis. One night, after I put Bradley, Matthew, and Elise to bed, I read through a pile of cards that had come in the mail. The cards, which came daily, were a reminder that this was really happening, that my son had leukemia and we needed a lot of prayer. I knelt at the edge of my

*Our Help*

bed and prayed for the help God promised to give me. I was overwhelmed with grief, but I clung to His words. *Our help is in the name of the Lord.* I cried and cried, but tried to stay quiet so I wouldn't awaken the three kids, peacefully asleep just down the hall. When the tears slowed, when I was too tired to weep anymore, I pulled myself up into bed, hoping for a few hours of sleep.

## Chapter 3

# Fear and Dread

*What I feared has come upon me;
what I dreaded has happened to me.
I have no peace, no quietness; I have
no rest, but only turmoil.*
**Job 3:25-26**

The other kids continued to be shuffled around to separate homes while Wes and I were at the hospital. Those who cared for Matthew voiced concerns about him. He still had that slight limp, and he was beginning to have difficulty standing up straight. We noticed Matthew leaning slightly forward when he walked. We couldn't pinpoint the problem and, for the most part, Matthew seemed content and happy, so we kept our focus on the real crisis. Even in crisis, though, we needed a break, so three days after Davis was diagnosed, Wes and I both came home from the hospital for

*Our Help*

a few hours while a friend stayed with Davis. We wanted to be together with Bradley, Matthew, and Elise to gauge how they were doing and calm any fears we might observe. We knew they missed us, and we missed them.

Our plan was to go on a bike ride. The kids were thrilled to do something "normal," and it was good for me, too. I was beginning to realize what a gift my regular routine was—I didn't want to complain about ordinary, mundane life ever again. The joy of riding bikes together was just as wonderful as a trip to Disney World—if not better! Bradley, Matthew, and Wes rode on ahead while I walked alongside little Elise, who pedaled her tricycle with great determination. She looked so sweet, and the fresh air felt so good. For the first time since the diagnosis, I felt a slight lift to my spirit. But as quickly as that feeling came, it was gone. Matthew, in tears, was walking toward me with his bike. He said his legs hurt when he rode, and he was frustrated he couldn't keep up with Daddy and Bradley. I scooped him up, but in my mind I was trying to figure out why he was acting this way. Was the stress in our family too much for him? Did he simply want more attention and time with me? I held him in my arms as we waited for Wes and Bradley to come back, and then we all slowly walked back to the house. We were disappointed; yet Wes and I were even more concerned about Matthew. What was happening to our tough, energetic four-year-old? We could tell he was struggling with something. Whatever it was, though, we were sure he would be better soon. Of course he'd bounce back.

But Matthew didn't bounce back. While Davis continued his stay in the hospital, Matthew continued to struggle at home. He missed a few days of preschool because he didn't feel well. He didn't have the words to describe how lethargic he felt from head to toe; sometimes when he was lying down, he didn't have the strength to lift his own arm. But he wasn't able to express this, and it made him very emotional. When Wes brought the kids to visit Davis in the hospital, Matthew became upset when it was time to leave. He wanted to be with me, but it was my turn to stay at the hospital with Davis. Separating Matthew from me was painfully hard and sad. With tears in his eyes, Matthew limped away, slightly dragging his foot. Just before he got into the elevator with Wes, Bradley, and Elise, he turned and gave me a half-hearted wave. When he turned away again, an eerie feeling rushed over me. Something was not right. I was experiencing the same feeling I'd had with Davis the week before. I was deeply troubled as I walked back into Davis' hospital room. Wes and I had to figure this out.

When my eyes saw little Davis smiling at me from his hospital bed, though, I was reminded of our more critical issue. We were encouraged with how well

Davis had responded to the initial chemotherapy, and even though we knew Davis' leukemia was serious, we were looking forward to the day he could come home. My uneasy feelings about Matthew were once again pushed aside.

In the middle of that week, the doctors told us Davis could go home on Saturday, ten days after diagnosis. We looked forward to his homecoming, but then, only a few days before it, Matthew started running a low-grade fever. When a child has leukemia and is receiving chemo, his immune system is weakened. Davis did not have the normal blood counts to ward off any type of flu or illness, and we had to be extremely careful whom he came in contact with—even a close family member. Matthew's fever was a sign of infection and a very real threat to Davis. So the day before Davis returned home, I took Matthew to see Dr. Betti. I also wanted to show Dr. Betti a new, painful-looking bruise Matthew had on his arm. I knew it was hurting him, but Matthew couldn't remember how he'd gotten it. Dr. Betti didn't have a clear explanation as to why his arm was so sore, but it was not broken, and he reminded me boys Matthew's age were bound to have bumps and bruises. He didn't see anything causing the fever, and so we were sent home with the encouraging words that Matthew would feel better in a day or two. Dr. Betti was very aware of our week with Davis, so naturally our conversation drifted to that topic. Despite Dr. Betti's calming words, I was disappointed we couldn't detect the source of the fever and we didn't know the reason for the pain in Matthew's arm, but these recurring, unsettled feelings were diverted once again in the excitement of bringing Davis home.

Saturday finally came, and we were all together! Bradley talked a mile a minute about school and everything that had happened the ten long days we'd been separated. Elise was back to her cute, imaginative games, enjoying real mommy-baby time with me and caring for her baby brother "Dabis." Matthew even seemed to feel better and perked up with the excitement in the house. It was absolutely wonderful to be home together. I can't explain it. It was like Christmas, and I felt it deeply. Little did I know how much I would need this short, happy respite.

Monday was our initial clinic day at Loyola's Cancer Treatment Center. This Center was a large, newly constructed building that had opened only a few weeks before we arrived. The pediatric nurses seemed friendly and upbeat. Diane and Mari Jo were the first oncology nurses to introduce themselves to me and guide me through the schedule. First, we saw Dr. Suarez. He did a routine check up and a blood draw. Once the staff knew Davis' blood counts, we were escorted over to the chemo/infusion room for infants, where Davis received his chemo over the next three hours. I was impressed with

*Our Help*

the doctors and nurses. They did their best to make clinic days as pleasant as possible. My new clinic schedule was Monday, Wednesday, and Friday for that week. I could do that. It was comforting to have a plan in place.

On Wednesday, October 5, my mom came over early in the morning to care for the other children while Davis and I went to his second clinic day. (Wes had to squeeze in a day here and there at the office.) Matthew had woken up sick again, with yet another fever, so I asked Mom to take him back to Dr. Betti. I was determined; this was the day we were going to figure this out. Dr. Betti must have felt the same. He decided to run a CBC on Matthew. He was shocked when he saw the results, so he did it again. "No, this can't be" must have been running through his mind. Poor Matthew! He hated having his finger poked, especially twice in one visit. When Dr. Betti got the second results, he questioned the accuracy of the CBC machine and asked my mom to have me call him as soon as I got home that afternoon.

By the time I arrived home, I was worried sick about Matthew, yet I was hoping Dr. Betti had discovered the problem and prescribed medication to address it. I really wanted Matthew to feel better. My mom gave me no reassuring news, though. She was noticeably worried and told me she sensed something was wrong by the way the nurses and doctors acted around her. I called

Dr. Betti right away and was told there was a possibility his CBC machine wasn't working properly. He wanted me to take Matthew to Central DuPage Hospital immediately for an accurate blood test. He would call me with the results. I had a feeling Dr. Betti already knew something, but he wouldn't tell me. What was it? I wouldn't let myself think the worst. No, of course not, *that* was inconceivable. *That* couldn't happen. I was sure of it.

Matthew—and I—made it through another blood test at our local hospital. Afterward, I gave him a piggyback ride all the way to the car to help him erase the memory of his third poke of the day. He was giggling as he and I bounced our way through the parking lot. I loved that sound; I needed to hear him laugh. His laughter counterbalanced the fear and dread I felt inside. We arrived back at our little Cape Cod house on Park Boulevard, and the phone rang almost immediately. I knew who it was. I knew it was never good to get results this quickly after a blood draw. I began shaking. Mom was pacing in the kitchen. I took one glance at her, sat down in the dining room chair, and answered the phone.

"Mrs. Wetherell, this is Dr. Betti. I have the results. I believe Matthew has what Davis has. I believe Matthew has leukemia, too."

A cold shiver ran through me.

"No, Dr. Betti, you can't be telling me this," I said, rejecting his diagnosis.

*Our Help*

"I'm so sorry, Beth. In all my 30 years of practice, I have never seen this before."

Silence. I began to unravel, unable to speak. How does your world stop ... again?

After a long pause, I whispered in the receiver, "I can't do this." This was too much to bear. Way too much. It was hard enough having one child with cancer. I couldn't repeat these past 13 days with another child of mine. They were both so young. This couldn't be happening.

"My staff and I will do whatever we can to help you. I've already called Davis' oncologist. He wants you to bring Matthew in tonight. They will run tests to confirm the diagnosis."

How was I supposed to go on from there? I wanted to crumple to the floor in a heap. I wanted my mom to hold me in her arms and tell me everything was going to be all right. But, once again, emotions had to be forced inward. They had to be stuffed down. As devastated as I was, I had to move. I had to get up out of that chair and step into the pain. I had four kids who needed me more than ever, and one of them had to be hospitalized immediately.

I called Wes. When I told him the news, he fell to the floor in his office and wept uncontrollably. Only a few minutes after I hung up the phone, my dear friend Sara Mascetti walked up our sidewalk, her arms filled with groceries. She thought she was coming to stock my refrigerator and pantry, but God brought her, at the perfect time, to support me, her devastated friend. I met her at the door and blurted out the awful news as fast as I could. I had told Wes and now Sara. It wasn't getting easier to say. Sara was stunned. Her whole body drooped, and she shook her head in disbelief. She stayed by my side and then Jeff arrived—again. Sara's husband, Perry, also a longtime friend, was the next one to join the solemn group. We waited together for Wes to get home. All of us had the same facial expression: shock and disbelief. It was a horrible, eerie, déjà vu moment.

I went upstairs to our bedroom where little Matthew was quietly watching TV with Bradley. I took a deep breath, bent down, took hold of his shoulders, and looked him in the eyes. "Matthew, I think we know why you haven't been feeling well. Dr. Betti thinks you might have leukemia just like Davis." The first thought that flashed through Matthew's mind was all the gifts Davis had received in the hospital and at home that week. Perry and Sara had generously given Davis his own little TV/Video player, thinking it would be a helpful distraction during the many hours he would spend resting in bed. Bradley and Matthew thought it was the coolest thing that Davis, a baby, had his own TV. *This* was what Matthew thought of when I mentioned the word "leukemia." He smiled and jumped up, his hands in the air, and then shouted, "Yippee! I get a TV!" He acted

*Our Help*

as if he had just won the lottery. That wasn't the reaction I expected, but, to be honest, I was relieved at his response. I couldn't imagine what I would have done if he'd started to cry. He would find out soon enough this was not a good thing. After our little talk, I walked directly into the bathroom and lost everything. I couldn't stop shaking. This was different than two weeks before because I knew now what we were facing. I just couldn't believe the nightmare was starting all over again.

Wes got home, and we thought through the impossible arrangements of leaving our kids again—this time with Davis home, with cancer, without us. We both felt we needed to be at the hospital with Matthew that first night. We were very quiet in the car as we headed, once again, to Loyola Hospital. I felt like I was going to faint or get sick, and I'm sure Wes felt the same way. But we couldn't say anything or do anything because Matthew was in the back of the car picking up on *everything*. He trusted us completely. He trusted us to be the parents we'd promised God we would be for him. He just wanted to "get all better." He had no idea what the next few days, weeks, and months would bring. Neither did Wes or I.

When we arrived at Loyola Hospital this time, we didn't go through the emergency room. Wes carried Matthew directly to the pediatric unit on the fourth floor. The nurses had a room and bed ready for him. The attending doctor came in shortly after we arrived and

*Fear and Dread*

told us they would run a few more tests on Matthew and have the results back to us late that evening. From their faces and voices, I could tell the doctor and the rest of the staff doubted our need to be there. They had seen this parental reaction before. Because Davis had leukemia, we worried that any little sniffle or bruise in our other children could also be a symptom of the disease. We were just over-reacting, overly sensitive parents. Totally understandable but irrational. Once further tests were done and they got the news they expected, leukemia would be ruled out and we could be discharged immediately. We, too, held onto a small amount of hope that somehow this was all a horrible mistake. Hadn't the nurses and doctors informed us leukemia wasn't contagious? Our kids could not "catch" leukemia from Davis. That made perfect sense. What was happening to our family did not.

Jeff and Lora came and stayed with us. Once Matthew was sound asleep, we walked across the hallway to a big conference room where the four of us could wait together for the test results but also remain close to Matthew. Finally, several tense hours later, the attending doctor returned. "We found blasts in Matthew's blood which confirm leukemia." Wes and I immediately fell into each other's arms and cried together this time. Within two weeks, we'd had two little boys diagnosed with leukemia. This was going to take some time to process. When we ran out of tears, we sat in that sterile room in silence. I rubbed my hands over my temples again and again; no one spoke for a long stretch of time.

Somehow, later that night, Jeff and Lora helped us decide sleeping arrangements. Wes stayed with Matthew, and Jeff and Lora took me home, where my mom was waiting up for me. We cried together. I knew this was so hard for her. Still grieving the loss of her husband, she was now watching her daughter and grandsons confront the same, life-threatening disease that took the love of her life. But as painful as this was for her, she was there for me, and she stayed in my pain with me. I kissed her good night, checked on my other sweet children, and crawled into bed completely exhausted and overwhelmed. What a day. I couldn't think beyond the moment. I just needed to sleep. But how could I after a day like this one? I closed my eyes, and in the stillness of the night, God poured out His peace by giving this mom the gift of sleep. On one of the worst nights of my life, He replenished my strength to face another day.

## Chapter 4

# Humble Yourselves

*Be not far from me, for trouble is near,
and there is none to help.*
**Psalm 22:11**

*Humble yourselves, therefore under the mighty
hand of God so that at the proper time he may
exalt you, casting all your anxieties on him,
because he cares for you.*
**1 Peter 5:6-7**

The next day, Dr. Suarez met with Wes and me in the same conference room we'd waited in the night before. Wes and I were seated at the long table when Dr. Suarez walked in, followed by four or five residents (Loyola is a teaching hospital). He confirmed Matthew's diagnosis to everyone gathered there and then walked

*Our Help*

to the large board in the front of the room. He barely made eye contact with us. He was fascinated that two brothers were diagnosed with the same cancer. He was even more intrigued that these two siblings were diagnosed *simultaneously*. He pointed out to the medical team present that Matthew and Davis could have been diagnosed with leukemia on the same day. The odds of this happening were remarkable. He had never seen or heard of this before.

As he continued his lecture, he went to the board and started writing out mathematical equations and *statistics*, thinking through the odds of this happening. I couldn't believe it. "What are you doing, Dr. Suarez?" I thought, "Those statistics are my children." Our lives were falling apart—and the doctor was teaching a class? He dispassionately continued. Wes and I stared at him in disbelief. I couldn't take any more. I dropped my head on the table and covered it with my hands. I didn't cry. I wailed. I didn't know I could make a noise like that. Wes tried to comfort me by rubbing my back. Dr. Suarez continued speaking, ignoring the anguish I was expressing directly in front of him. I was done. I got up from the table and left the room. I didn't care if Dr. Suarez was still talking.

I walked across the hall and into Matthew's room. Tears continued to roll down my cheeks as I watched him sleep. He'd had such a hard, scary night. He was so sick, so worn out. My hands clenched tight on the bed

*Humble Yourselves*

rails, and I looked up to the ceiling and quietly cried out to God. "What have I done? Tell me, what have I done to make you so mad at me?" Just then Dad Wetherell walked in. He came over to my side and placed his loving, strong arms around my shoulders. He didn't say anything; he simply stood in silence with me, both of us looking at Matthew. But his presence gave me the strength to continue with my honest, private questions to God. "What happened here, God? Are you punishing me? What did I do? God, I want to know. I've been a good, Christian girl all my life. Why didn't you protect my children?" I felt betrayed and abandoned by God. I was so disappointed and so confused.

Later that afternoon, while Matthew was taking a nap, the pediatric social worker came in and stayed with me for over an hour. Most of the time we sat in silence as she observed my emotional state. She had a calming, supportive presence, and this quieted my soul and gave me the space I needed to think about the morning and the questions I had for God. Maybe I was asking God the wrong questions. Rain falls on everyone. In the same way, suffering falls on everyone, too, whether they are good or bad. No one gets a pass from pain or heartache. Suffering is a part of life. Instead of asking God, "Why me?" and doubting His goodness, I started thinking the more accurate question was "Why not?" Just a week earlier, while in the hospital with Davis, I'd watched a

*Our Help*

news report on TV about a family that had been driving to Milwaukee when a taillight assembly fell off a truck in front of them. Their van hit this and burst into flames. The parents tried to rescue their children but were unable to save any of them. All six of the children in the van died, and the parents were badly burned. The Willis family lost six kids within a few minutes. This tragedy and my own time in the PICU opened my eyes to how quickly something can go wrong. I was developing a different perspective about life, one I'd already known in theory but hadn't before experienced: this world is not safe. Really sad things can happen to anyone. At some point in life, we will all find ourselves in a difficult and potentially dangerous situation. Davis and Matthew were in danger, and we needed help. We desperately needed help.

As I continued to process these weighty thoughts, the Holy Spirit reminded me of God's promise to me. He would be *our help*. My help was in His name, in all His attributes, in His character, in *Him*. This realization amazed me. In my time of need, I wanted to run *to* Him, not away *from* Him. He could be trusted with my pain. He understood. He cared. He knew my need before *I* knew my need. That afternoon was the start of me becoming brutally honest with God. My conversations with Him became raw and specific. I knew He could handle my prayers. I shared with Him my

*Humble Yourselves*

emotions, fears, everything. Prepackaged, impersonal prayers would not suffice in this situation, only truth between a very frightened young mom and her very awesome God.

We learned more about Matthew's leukemia that day. Like Davis, he had Acute Lymphoblastic Leukemia (ALL), but since he was four years old, his prognosis was better. The doctors explained to us that Matthew had a 70-80% chance of survival. He would need to endure 3 ½ years of chemotherapy, but if he didn't relapse, he could, someday, be cured of this awful disease. This was somewhat encouraging, but those odds didn't really comfort me. There was still a 30% chance my little boy could die of this cancer, and this completely terrified me. At the same time, we continued to learn more about Davis' leukemia. He had so much going against him. His age and white blood count at diagnosis pointed to a much more aggressive leukemia than Matthew's, even though they were both ALL. We learned there are many types of childhood leukemia, each one demanding a slightly different protocol regarding chemotherapy, and each one with a different prognosis. Matthew's leukemia fell into the "good prognosis" category, and Davis' fell into the "poor prognosis" category. Neither of them satisfied me. I wanted them both in the "100%, absolutely, positively, we can cure them" category.

*Our Help*

On Matthew's third day in the hospital, Wes stayed with him while I took Davis to the Cancer Treatment Center for his third day of clinic. My friend Gail came with me while other friends and family cared for Elise and Bradley. It was very helpful to have Gail with me at the clinic—this was just too hard to do without Wes. Davis was not only receiving chemo through his line that day, he was also having a spinal tap. This is a procedure performed in the lower spine to see if any cancer is in the spinal fluid. If cancer cells are found in the spinal fluid, then the leukemia has spread to the central nervous system. During the spinal tap, the doctor will often administer a chemotherapy drug because this is the only way chemo can get to the brain.

As the boys continued their treatment, they frequently had another medical procedure called a bone marrow aspiration, in which the doctor takes marrow from the hipbone to detect any leukemia cells forming in the marrow. As I learned more about these procedures, I understood that the science behind them was fascinating, but for us, they were simply personal and traumatic. Each time my boys underwent a procedure, my stomach was in knots waiting for the results, since the results from either of these tests could extend hope for survival or extinguish it. Life and death hung in the balance each time. But on this day in early October, the day of Davis' first spinal, I didn't yet understand the

*Humble Yourselves*

gravity of the test. All I knew was that it was another unknown, and it was frightening.

While Davis received his chemo, I was trying to figure out how to tell the nurses the terrible news of Matthew's diagnosis. I didn't know how to start the conversation. Everything I thought of sounded so surreal and awkward: "Good morning! Hey, guess what? I have two kids with cancer—imagine that?!" While Nurse Diane was checking Davis' central line, I moved in close to her and whispered, "Our son Matthew is in the hospital. He has leukemia, too." I assumed she didn't know. Diane didn't make eye contact but gently put her hand on my shoulder. She softly said, "I know, Beth." She wasn't shocked, and her calm response was a relief. Nurse Diane was incredible, and I knew Matthew would like her.

After chemo, we went to the procedure room where they prepared Davis for his spinal. It was a terribly cold, sterile room without a shred of comfort in it. Then I spotted a smiley sticker stuck on a syringe deposit box on the wall. I stared at that smiley sticker and thought how odd it was to see a happy smile in a place where smiles never happen. Gail and I tried to keep the conversation light. After the nurses sedated Davis and positioned his listless body into a tight ball on the cold table, Dr. Suarez began the spinal. He pushed a large needle into the center of my baby's lower back, and I turned away. I refused to watch any more. When it was all over, I quickly wrapped Davis in blankets and rocked him as he slowly came out of sedation. I didn't want to let go of him. He was safe with me.

Then I remembered that as soon as Davis was completely awake, I needed to head back to the hospital to see Matthew. The hospital building was close to the Cancer Treatment Center, so Gail dropped me off at the hospital entrance before heading home with Davis. It was so hard to separate from my baby after such a tough procedure, but I had no choice. I forced a smile, kissed his sweet forehead, and waved good-bye to him as they drove away.

When I got off the elevator on the pediatric floor and turned the corner to walk down the hall to Matthew's room, I was startled to see him sitting straight up in his bed, out in the middle of the hallway. Wes was standing by his side. I smiled at Matthew's sweet face as I got closer and then looked at Wes.

"Where's Matthew going, Wes?"

"We're going down to surgery to get his central line put in. I didn't want to tell you until you got up here."

We decided Wes would stay back in the room since some good friends from the Covenant Church, where Wes grew up, had stopped by for a visit. I was glad I'd arrived before Matthew headed to surgery. I wanted to be with him. I walked alongside his bed as we made

*Humble Yourselves*

our way to the pre-op area. Matthew was wheeled into a holding area where the nurses gave him a medicine called silly syrup. Silly syrup helps children relax so they can easily separate from their mom or dad when it's time to head to the operating room. It also makes kids, well, silly. Matthew indeed got silly! We laughed together, again and again, over the same dumb joke, and sang the B-I-B-L-E song five hundred times. Matthew would mix up his sentences and then giggle because of how funny he sounded. I loved hearing him laugh.

After an hour or so—nothing, absolutely nothing, goes quickly in a hospital—two men dressed in green scrubs arrived to take Matthew to surgery. I was also wearing scrubs, a cap, and mask. I walked alongside Matthew's bed until we came to an extremely long hallway. The nurses tried to explain to my four-year-old that they were going to take him to a special room, and Mommy would be with him when he was done. Even though he was heavily sedated, Matthew did not want to go without me. He started to cry and stretched his arms toward me. I held back tears and said, "You'll be okay, and I'll be right by your side when you wake up." After a few reassuring kisses, he stopped protesting and quietly allowed them to roll his bed down the excruciatingly long hallway. We watched each other as the distance grew between us. The nurses told him to lie down on the bed, but he stubbornly refused. He sat straight up, facing me as they wheeled him backward down the hall. He never took his big, sad, brown eyes off me. I had to clench my muscles tight to stop myself from running down that hallway, snatching my son off the bed, and holding him in my arms. Finally, the bed turned the corner, and he was out of my sight.

My hand was still in waving position when that very long, narrow hallway became quiet and eerily empty. No one was around. I was alone. I wasn't prepared to be alone, especially alone with my thoughts. I couldn't avoid the truth: I had two children with cancer; one had undergone a spinal tap that morning; the other was in surgery to insert a central line; and I couldn't be with either one of them. I'd had to say goodbye to both of them and send them off in someone else's care. A large lump started swelling in my throat, and then the trembling began. The weight of it hit me once again with tremendous force, and I sobbed. A nurse heard me and quickly came into the hall. She tried to console me as she helped me remove my surgical clothes. When they were off, she handed me a large box of Kleenex. In between sobs, I mumbled something about this being my second child having central line surgery in two weeks, and her response told me she knew my story. By this time, the tears were coming harder and faster than I could wipe them away. I could hardly see as I made my way back up to the fourth floor. I stood in a walkway that overlooked the parking lot. I was overwhelmed with sorrow and fear. I couldn't stop the tears, the deep ache, the shaking—it seemed it would never end. Nurses, doctors, patients, and families walked by, not saying a word. They respected my space to cry. Most understood. Many people cried out in that walkway. They, too, had their own tragic stories.

Grief and fear were common emotions on the pediatric floor. Most of the children on this floor weren't there to get their tonsils out or mend a broken finger. Each room held very ill or seriously injured children with frightened, traumatized parents and extended family by their side. Over time I observed other families experiencing incredible grief. I saw a mother crumple to the floor in the hallway when she received word her child had just died. I watched for a minute or two and then headed back into my own hospital room, praying, *"Please, Lord, don't take my boys away from me. Please let them be a part of our family; please heal their little bodies. Please don't let them die."*

I stayed with Matthew overnight after his central line surgery. We decided it would be best for Wes to sleep at home because Bradley and Elise were scheduled to see Dr. Betti first thing in the morning. Both pediatric oncologists thought it wise to test Bradley and Elise, to make sure they didn't have leukemia. Wes knew there was no way I could go into that office again. I was terrified to think that all my kids could have leukemia.

*Our Help*

That night before their appointments, I tried to sleep, but it was almost impossible. I was so nervous. I must have dozed off at some point because I had a nightmare. All four of my children were standing in front of me, with their backs up against a wall. Their sad faces were sickly white and all had gruesome central lines protruding out of their chests. How sick, how awful. I awoke in fear and began praying that this nightmare would never come true. I continued praying until the morning light streamed through the hospital room, awakening Matthew. Even as I helped him eat breakfast and change clothes, my mind was constantly on Bradley and Elise. I kept looking at the clock, praying, checking the clock, praying. I prayed at the time of their appointment. I prayed as I visualized Bradley and Elise getting their blood drawn. I knew they were scared. I kept praying. I was terribly anxious of what might be.

The phone rang quicker than I'd expected. Before I could say hello, Wes yelled, "Everything is good! Bradley and Elise's tests came back normal!" I finally exhaled. My fear subsided for a moment. I did not have four children with leukemia.

But I did have two.

## Chapter 5

# Grace

*Draw near to God and He will draw near to you.*
**James 4:8**

*But he said to me, "My grace is sufficient for you, for my power is made perfect in your weakness."*
**2 Corinthians 12:9**

Matthew stayed in the hospital for a week after his initial diagnosis. When he was feeling up to it, he could take a trip to the playroom or join in on an activity out in the hall. A small petting zoo showed up one day to cheer up the kids on the floor. Matthew also enjoyed having visitors his age. His cousins Chris and Nicki came to see him along with Aunt Lisa and Uncle Reid (Wes' brother). Their presence put a smile on Matthew's face. Jeff and Lora brought their son, Josh, who was a close friend of Matthew's, and Bradley visited a few times when he wasn't in school. Sadly, Matthew wasn't up for visitors or fun activities very often.

The medicine was starting to have an effect on his carefree, happy disposition. He especially struggled with the oral medicine he was asked to take. He tried his best. He would get up enough four-year-old courage to swallow a pill, only to throw it back up immediately, along with whatever food and drink were in his stomach. This was a huge problem and an extreme stress on all of us. We understood why Matthew had a difficult time with this skill; many adults do. But we also had intense pressure building within us: it was so important for Matthew to have those meds in his body. It was, in our minds, a matter of life and death. Some of the nurses didn't help either. A few started threatening Matthew, which only made things worse. Within a few days it was clear: the combination of Matthew and meds was not gonna' happen. We tried everything to cover up those nasty pills—yogurt, ice cream, pudding, pop, applesauce . . . You name it, we tried it. No, No, NO! I felt so bad for Matthew; he was being asked to do something that made him throw up. Who would agree to that? Prednisone had the worst taste, and Matthew was supposed to take it three times a day. It wouldn't be that bad if he swallowed it, but he only knew how to chew pills. He also had to take an antibiotic called Bactrim. He hated the "kids" version of that, too. Wes and I were at our wit's end trying to deal with this problem.

One night, I asked the nurses to help. I thought if I weren't in the room, it might be easier for the attending nurses to get Matthew to take his meds. Lora was visiting me, and when it was medication time, she and I went out in the hall together. We waited as two nurses began coaxing Matthew. Within a few seconds, though, he was protesting and beginning to cry. The nurses became more forceful, to the point of threatening Matthew. His cries grew to hysterical screams. Both Lora and I knew the nurses had crossed the line, and this challenge was over. I rushed in and asked the nurses to leave. Matthew was so upset he threw up again. I felt terrible. *I shouldn't have let this happen*, I thought. Lora and I got everything cleaned up, but Matthew was still traumatized. His small body shook, and he gasped for air every few minutes. I had to do something to help him. I crawled in bed with him, wrapped my arms around his trembling body, and held him as close as I could. I began to sing, very quietly "Jesus loves me, this I know." Within 15 minutes or so, Matthew calmed down. His little body slowly relaxed, and he fell asleep in my arms. Not wanting to disturb him, Lora and I didn't say another word. Tears in our eyes, we just stared at each other while the room grew dark for the night.

*Our Help*

The next morning, Wes and I decided we were going to be upbeat and positive about Matthew's meds. We needed to be more encouraging. So we invented a fun little game to help the medicine go down. We acted goofy, hoping to distract him as he placed the pill in his mouth. But within minutes, the pill-taking process escalated out of control again, and Matthew was hopping out of bed, grabbing his IV pole and limping into the tiny, narrow bathroom to throw up. As he vomited into the toilet, I stood behind him, holding his IV pole, watching him. Wes was just behind me, trying to help as well. What came next—what we later named my *official* meltdown—was unannounced. Without any warning, I became someone I didn't recognize, behaving in ways I had never imagined myself capable of. I turned to Wes and started kicking his legs, beating his chest as I cried out in anguish. I attacked him as if he was the problem. More accurately, I attacked him as if he was the cancer. I wanted it gone; I wanted to fight it off so Matthew would not suffer any more. Poor Wes—he absorbed it all. He understood. All the stress, grief, fear, anxiety, trauma . . . It all finally came to a boiling point, and I erupted.

And then it got worse. When Matthew finished throwing up, he saw me crying, and he started crying, too. "It's all my fault, Mommy, it's all my fault!" he sobbed. I hadn't thought I could feel any worse, but when I heard

*Grace*

those words from my four-year-old son—with cancer—standing next to the toilet, leaning on his own IV pole in exhaustion, my devastation went even deeper. I was at an all-time low, utterly in despair. What was happening to me? I was racked with guilt and shame for the way I'd behaved toward Wes—and for doing it in front of my child.

Late that night, I sat in the dark next to Matthew as he slept. I listened to the clicking monitors and relived the past two days. I felt like such a failure as a mom and wife. My life was out of control. In the quiet of the night, I prayed, "I need you, Lord. Please help me." Once again, God drew near. He reminded me *He* was in control and I could trust him even when everything was horrible—even when I made it worse. His grace *would always be* sufficient in my weakest moments, in Wes' and Matthew's weakest moments—in all our weakest moments. What a beautiful truth the Apostle Paul attests to in the book of Corinthians. Leaning on God's strength gave me hope. A flicker of hope rose to the surface from my defeated, broken state. My circumstances didn't change, but my heart certainly did.

His grace given to me that evening was simply amazing. He gave me strength and a determination to protect my kids. I realized it was not helpful to Wes or my family if I continued to break down. I understood I would be overwhelmed at times, but I could call on

*Our Help*

God in those moments to strengthen me and give me courage. When I was weak, I could lean on him, confident that His powerful hand would uphold me and help me. If God equipped me to be a mother of four children, then he would equip and empower me to be a mom of two children with cancer. He could do this. "Our help *is* in the name of the Lord, who made heaven and earth." *Thank You so much, Lord, for revealing Your strength to me when I had nothing. Thank You for a little bit of hope. Thank You for Your grace—it was just what I needed.*

The next morning was Monday, and the pediatric floor of the teaching hospital was hopping with doctors, specialists, residents, nurses, play therapists, and social workers! Dr. Hayani was scheduled to check up on Matthew, and I was ready. I had been given strength from above. I wanted Matthew to feel as safe as possible in the hospital, and it was my job to communicate his needs clearly to the hospital staff and protect him from any unnecessary trauma. He might be under the care of doctors and nurses, but I still played a vital part in his health and recovery. So before anyone could come near my son, or any of my kids for that matter, they would have to go through me first. I became the protective "mama bear" for the Wetherell boys on the pediatric floor at Loyola Hospital, and it made a difference.

After Dr. Hayani finished checking Matthew, I asked if I could speak with him out in the hall. The residents followed us. I told him about the two horrible experiences we'd had with Matthew that weekend and expressed how traumatic it was for all of us. I told him I was very concerned about Matthew's emotional health and it was time to think of other ways to get the medicine into him. I was relieved to see Dr. Hayani so concerned; he understood, asked me which nurses were involved, and apologized over and over for all the trouble. Then he said words that were music to my ears: "Don't worry, Beth. Matthew can receive his meds through his central line. He doesn't have to take them orally. Eventually he will need to learn to swallow pills, but let's not push it right now. He's been through enough." He placed his hand on my shoulder and gave me a reassuring smile. He would take care of our immediate pill problem—what a huge relief! He was on our side, on Matthew's side. I gained a new perspective on Dr. Hayani that morning, and this allowed me to see how much he cared for his patients and their families. He treated his patients as if they were his own children. We've thanked God over and over for this wise, compassionate doctor.

What a difference a day made. I had turned the corner. I had come to understand I needed to be an advocate for my sons. I needed to protect them. I had learned I had a voice in the hospital and I could use it to speak up for them—I *had* used it. I had a new sense of confidence I'd not had before. God stepped in. His strength gave me power. I had none and He offered His. What amazing grace.

## Chapter 6

# A Strong Tower

*When I am afraid, I put my trust in you.*
**Psalm 56:3**

*The name of the LORD is a strong tower;
the righteous man runs into it and is safe.*
**Proverbs 18:10**

Life with two kids undergoing chemotherapy was beginning to sink in. We would be in this routine for months, if not years. Practically, I wondered, "How is this going to work?" Matthew and Davis had to be at the cancer treatment center almost daily. Either Matthew was receiving chemo, or Davis was, or both. Other times, Davis needed to be at the clinic while Matthew was in the hospital, or the other way around. I also had to get Bradley off to school

*Our Help*

in the morning, oversee Elise's needs, and allow Wes to go into work as much as possible. We appreciated how supportive our church was with childcare, but I knew this arrangement would not work long term. Elise couldn't be bounced around from one house to another every day. It was too confusing and unsettling for her. I worried about Bradley, too; after school, he was being shuffled around like Elise. They both needed more stability.

Someone suggested I hire an Au Pair. Maybe that was the answer. I called a church friend, Pat, who had an Au Pair business and asked her how it worked. As she described the Au Pair position and the commitments we would have to make, I realized this idea wouldn't work for our situation. I hung up the phone discouraged. As I sat at the table, staring out the window, wondering what to do next, the phone rang. It was Pat calling back; she had an idea. A young lady with Au Pair experience had recently left Pat's business. She was from Ireland, was recently married, and she had a young boy. She was also planning on staying in the States. She lived close, in Carol Stream, a city just north of Glen Ellyn. The best thing about her was she was looking for a day job. Pat highly recommended her as one who could work well with our unique circumstances. She cooked, cleaned, and could work nights and weekends when needed. I got off the phone with a renewed sense of hope. This

*A Strong Tower*

time hope took the form of a young lady from Ireland named Tara Krisch.

I called Tara the very next day and explained everything. Amazingly, she didn't decline immediately. She actually seemed interested in the idea. We set up a time to meet. Tara came over a day or two later, and I interviewed her and told her our story. It all seemed terribly surreal to talk about central lines, hospital and clinic visits, and overnight stays at the hospital. At one point I did caution her this could be a sad job—leukemia is a serious disease. It was hard to get those words out. It was even harder to look Tara in the eyes and watch as she grasped what I was saying. She understood, and her compassionate response was comforting. She was sympathetic to our situation and, best of all, she seemed up for the task. The next day, as Wes and I returned home from a long day at the clinic, I called Tara on our new car phone and hired her. She was able to start immediately. Looking back, I am still amazed at how simply and beautifully it worked out. Tara was another gift from God. He was fulfilling his promise. I could not have survived the next eight months without her in my life. I needed help, and God provided Tara.

Any parents who hear their child has leukemia, no matter what type, are devastated. We were deeply concerned for both Davis and Matthew, but initially Davis' cancer was our greater concern because the input

*Our Help*

we'd received from the doctors about him was very troubling. The chances of survival dropped significantly in children diagnosed before age one. Davis was 11 months at diagnosis. Also, chances of survival dropped in children with an extremely high white blood count. That, too, described Davis. Then, one month after diagnosis, the chromosome results came back on Davis' leukemic cell, and we got the worst news yet. Davis had a unique translocation with the 4th and 11th chromosomes. The doctors called it a t(4;11) translocation. What did this mean? Bottom line, it meant Davis had little or no chance of survival. The medical books and articles describe the prognosis of children who have leukemia with the t(4;11) abnormality as dismal. Dismal. When I read that, I wondered how the doctors came up with that horrible description. "Dismal" didn't sound like a medical term to me; it sounded hopeless. "Dismal" sounded like a cure was impossible.

Dr. Hayani broke the t(4;11) news to me on a Friday while I was at the clinic with little Matthew for his chemo. I kept bouncing Matthew on my lap, and Dr. Hayani kept talking, but I didn't hear anything after "less than 5 percent chance of survival." Finally I stopped him. I wrapped my arms around Matthew, looked at Dr. Hayani, and whispered, "I can't take anymore. That's enough." I was determined not to fall apart again in front of Matthew. Dr. Hayani said we would talk more about this in detail on Monday. That evening Wes and I somehow got through the bedtime routine with all the kids and then confronted the reality of this new and terrifying diagnosis. We were one month in, and I was already weary of fighting this awful disease. Cancer is like riding a sickening roller-coaster. Our hopes would climb one day and drop like a brick the next—it all depended on what the doctors were telling us or how Matthew and Davis were feeling.

The news about Davis' chromosomes was a hard blow in our fight with leukemia. Wes and I tried and tried to think of something we could do. Nothing. Over and over I pushed away the awful thoughts of Davis dying. I never played out the details completely—my mind wouldn't let me go there, yet the threat was real, and I knew it. Wes and I brainstormed about another way to treat our baby. There had to be another option. We knew chemotherapy alone wouldn't cure Davis' leukemia, so we thought maybe a bone marrow transplant (BMT) would. We were waiting to hear if Davis' cancer was in remission (the usual time frame for this is one month after diagnosis). We knew if it was, he would be a good candidate for a BMT. We thought this was a good idea to propose to the doctors.

At the clinic on Monday, I looked for the right opportunity to share our ideas with Dr. Hayani, but before I could get the suggestion out, he began sharing the exact same plan with me! He, too, had been thinking about options all weekend. He informed me that high-risk leukemia patients like Davis were unlikely to be cured using chemotherapy alone and these patients have a better chance of survival if they receive a bone marrow transplant. The chance of survival increases if the patient is in remission during the time of the transplant. God was pulling us out of despair once again. We had a new plan. Dr. Hayani said the next step was to test our healthy kids, Bradley and Elise, to see if one of them had the same type of bone marrow. There was a twenty-five percent chance that one sibling's marrow would match another sibling's. If either Bradley or Elise was a match for Davis, then his chance for survival increased significantly to forty or fifty percent. Dr. Hayani got up to leave the examining room but then turned back. He smiled warmly at me and said, "Davis deserves better."

Yes, he does.

Within a few days we found out both Matthew and Davis were in remission. This was great news! Their bodies had responded favorably to the chemotherapy. Our family, friends, and church rejoiced with us. We had much to celebrate after weeks of discouraging news. We were given more time together as a family.

And more family time is truly treasured time.

## Chapter 7

# Wait in Hope

*We wait in hope for the Lord; he is our help and our shield. In him our hearts rejoice, for we trust in his holy name. May your unfailing love rest on us, O Lord, even as we put our hope in you.*
**Psalm 33:20-22**

The following week our entire family drove down to Loyola Cancer Treatment Center. Bradley got the day off school. He was happy, but he did not yet know missing school would involve a "poke." Jeff and Lora came with us to assist. Being together is usually fun, but this time, not so much. Davis and Matthew had clinic visits with chemo, and Bradley and Elise were getting their blood drawn to see if one of them was a match for Davis. It ended up being a tough day for all our kids. The needle frightened Elise, but we were done quickly since she was so light and easy to hold. Bradley, however, fought as hard as he could against the inevitable. We found out he was pretty strong for his age. He remembered all too clearly his kindergarten shots, and that was something he did not want to relive. We tried calm reason and soothing tones, but nothing worked. Two nurses and I had to restrain him while a third nurse drew his blood. We were all a sweaty mess when it was over. I soothed Bradley and felt a flare of anger in my gut: this cancer was affecting all our kids.

The nurses also comforted Bradley and Elise, providing them with yummy snacks and a trip to the treasure box. These nurses were so kind to my family, and I was quickly becoming friends with many of them. I actually started looking forward to clinic days. It sounds odd to say that, but it was, at times, fun to be there. This was another of God's surprising blessings.

Bradley's and Elise's blood was sent to the lab to determine if it was a perfect match for Davis. It would be three to four weeks before we heard the results. While we waited, we had other challenges to face. Matthew still needed to learn how to take his meds. I knew the time was fast approaching when his protocol called for oral meds to be taken. The nurses said the pills were extremely bitter, so chewing them was not an option. One of our biggest, practical prayer requests for Matthew (our strong-willed and now sick son) was that he would learn to swallow a pill. God helped us over this hurdle by giving me a bit of mom-wisdom. I bought some candy that Bradley and Matthew loved and that, more importantly, were very small—Nerds! They didn't have the exact shape as pills but the size was similar. Using the motivation of a little sibling competition, I asked Bradley and Matthew to come into the kitchen for a special challenge. I showed them both the Nerds. "I want to see if you can do something fun! I want to see if you can place one Nerd on your tongue, take a drink of water, and swallow it without chewing. If you can, I will give you a handful to eat. Now, who thinks they can do it?" Both Bradley and Matthew loved challenges, and this one involved candy—perfect. They both did it successfully the first time!

I was ecstatic that Matthew swallowed it without gagging or throwing up, but I knew better than to relate it to medicine at this time or he might have felt I'd tricked him. We continued this little game every day for about a week or two. Some of the Nerd candy pieces were getting pretty big, yet Bradley and Matthew continued to swallow them easily. Then I took a leap and switched to kids chewable Tylenol. Those yummy pills did not threaten Matthew, and when I asked if he could swallow the Tylenol pill just like the Nerds, he confidently and quickly washed it down his throat. I told Matthew since he could swallow those big pills, he could easily swallow any meds at the clinic or hospital. The connection was

*Our Help*

made, and Matthew was proud of his accomplishment. He seemed confident about swallowing pills, and we were hopeful we would not have to repeat the horrible oral-meds experience again.

A few weeks later, the moment of truth came. Matthew was beginning a new phase of chemo that required oral prednisone and oral methotrexate. I was so nervous inside as I held out the six, tiny, blue, bitter tablets. I could tell Matthew was nervous, too. His hands shook as he took them from me, but he did it! Victory! What a really happy moment for us! Matthew was so proud of himself, and his problems with pills never returned. Later in his treatment, he often had to take some pretty nasty meds orally, and he always downed them like a champ. I was also very grateful for Bradley's part in the breakthrough—what a big accomplishment for these young boys!

The steroid prednisone really messed up our chemo boys. They craved food, especially salty, carb-filled foods—all the time. I would put a big bowl of spaghetti in front of Davis, and he would devour it with his little hands, shoving it into his mouth as fast as possible. Matthew was no different; he was hungry all the time. He went to bed eating cereal, literally eating while he fell asleep. Then he would wake in the middle of the night still hungry. He would get me out of bed, and the two of us would go downstairs where he would eat another

*Wait in Hope*

bowl or two. We eventually left a full bowl next to his bed so he didn't have to get up in the night, and I could get some sleep. After three weeks on this steroid, Davis and Matthew had the chubbiest cheeks, and they were both busting through their clothes. I had to buy new ones to accommodate their growing waistlines.

Prednisone also affected Matthew emotionally. He had scary mood swings and difficulty coping with the slightest problem. For example, if his shoelace came untied, he'd sob uncontrollably. We videotaped a family dinner one night, and it happened to be a time when Matthew was under the influence of prednisone. We caught on tape how seriously upset Matthew became when he didn't get enough butter on his roll. "Not enough butter!" he cried, while his hand holding the roll shook. We felt so bad for him. There were times we had to hold him in a restraining hug as he kicked and screamed through a difficult moment (or hour). He also experienced the suicidal feelings that are another side effect of the drug. One time he told me he felt like putting sharp knives in his chest. Those were unpredictable and scary days for our young Matthew, but God protected him. He tenderly and lovingly watched over him. Nothing slipped by those divine eyes.

With Tara working for us, we fell into a somewhat predictable routine. I remembered what our social worker, Marilyn Reinish, at Loyola had told us just a day after Davis' diagnosis. "Welcome to your new norm," she said. She told us we were starting a new journey; we would never return to the old. I didn't like hearing those words, but she was right. Marilyn was another wonderful blessing to Wes and me. She had a warm, welcoming way of speaking to us, and her smile is one I will never forget. She was with me during my darkest moments, graciously comforting me along the way. She asked the tough questions and reminded Wes and me that our marriage was at risk by having two kids with cancer and if we needed help, she was there for us. We already knew of one husband and wife from the clinic who were struggling in their marriage, and within a year, we would see two sets of parents divorce while their children continued to go through chemotherapy. The stress was too much. Marilyn's proactive warnings and check-ins protected our marriage. Our dear kids needed us to be united, and we were committed to each other. But I do have one story to confess that shows how dangerous stress can be for a marriage.

One day, Sara and Gail came to the hospital to stay with Davis so Wes and I could "change the guard," something we often did. This time it involved my going home to stay with the other kids while Wes went to the hospital to spend the night with Davis. This particular day had been very long and hard, probably for both of us for different reasons, and we were annoyed with each other.

*Wait in Hope*

Within minutes—thankfully while the kids were in the basement playing—Wes and I got into a disagreement. I have no memory of what it was about, but I remember what followed it. Suddenly I was in Wes' face, speaking harshly. My cutting words were more than Wes could take, so he pushed me down on the couch. It wasn't a hard push, just enough to get my attention, but I got even angrier. I jumped back up and continued to tell him a thing or two, so he forced me back down on the couch. That pushed me over the edge. I popped up and swiped my fingernails across Wes' face.

This shocked both of us. Horrified, I burst into tears. I ran out the door and down the block. It was cold and dreary, but I kept running. I had never hit or scratched anyone before in my life. (The one exception was when I was little and scratched my bother Paul because he wouldn't stop tickling me.) I continued to run. The fresh air felt good, like it was blowing away my anger, my guilt, my shame. Then reality hit: I was not a runner. My feet were starting to hurt, I was out of breath, and I was getting cold. What a stupid thing I'd done! I couldn't keep running away. Davis needed his daddy at the hospital. I needed to turn around and go home. When I stepped back into the house, I was relieved to see compassion on Wes' face—along with three bloody streaks across his cheek. I felt terrible, but together we were able to reconcile. We held each other and re-affirmed the bedrock of our marriage. Our family situation would at times get the best of us, but love would always prevail. For us, there was no other option. We were in this together. That was the commitment we'd made to each other and to God the day we got married, and nothing was going to break that.

After Wes left, I called Davis' hospital room. My friend answered. "Wes is on his way," I said, "and, by the way, please do me a huge favor. Don't ask Wes what happened to his face. We're good." No questions were asked, and no judgments were made, and I am still thankful for the close friends who walked this journey with us and supported us through thick and thin.

A few weeks later, my mom and my sister-in-law, Jean, came along with me to the clinic. Friends and family often went with me; clinic days were long (9 a.m. to 6 p.m. most days) and having company helped the time pass for both Matthew and me. My mom would sit and play board games with Matthew while his infusion machine pumped the cancer-killing medicine into his body. She was a wonderful distraction for him. Her smile calmed him, and her teasing made him laugh. This day was turning out to be just another long day at the clinic, filled with lab work, doctor consults, and a chemo infusion. But as we were finishing up late that afternoon, Diane said she had some very important news for us: the bone marrow results on our two

*Wait in Hope*

healthy kids. She needed to call Dr. Hayani to find out if he wanted to come over and tell us the results or if she could. This was enormous news—incredibly stressful but also filled with the possibility of hope. Time came to a screeching halt. I watched every move, every expression Diane made. I listened intently to every word she said and tried my best to hear what Dr. Hayani was saying back to her. Diane's tone and slight smile suggested we had good news—could we really have a match? Mom, Jean, and I froze, holding our breath for the anticipated news. When Diane hung up the phone, she quickly turned to us and announced, "Elise is a match!"

I cannot describe the exhilaration I felt when I heard those words! Davis had a match from his family! Our delicate, little daughter, Elisabeth Hope, was going to be part of the *hope* Davis so desperately needed. Her marrow did not match Bradley's marrow or even Matthew's marrow. Her marrow matched Davis'. We were greatly relieved and thrilled at the same time. Psalm 139 describes in great detail God's intimate knowledge of our bodies, His deliberate and careful creation of us. This day, He was revealing something He'd known all along: Elise and Davis had the same type of marrow. Marrow is considered a match when the donor and the recipient have the same Human Leukocyte Antigen (HLA) markers or proteins in their cells. Doctors can determine this through a detailed blood test. A minimum of six

*Our Help*

HLA matched markers was necessary for a successful transplant outcome. Elise matched Davis' marrow in all six.

We were grateful—and we were amazed. The complexity of our bodies, and specifically our bone marrow, is awe-inspiring. We are truly fearfully and wonderfully made, just as the psalmist declared. We are God's creation, and He knows every detail about us. He created Davis. He knew Davis would have cancer. He knew what Davis would need and how He, God, would help us. Two years before Davis was born, he created our sweet Elise with beautiful, wonderful, hope-giving marrow to match her future younger brother's. Incredible! Wes would often say to people, "Even before we knew we had a problem, God had already given us hope—Elisabeth Hope." Yes, there is no doubt our God is an all-knowing, all-powerful, sovereign God. He was and is in all the details of life because He creates and sustains it all.

We were very thankful Matthew's ALL was a type of leukemia that responded well to chemo. We were hopeful he would not need a bone marrow transplant, but we also knew relapse was still possible. This worried us since he didn't have a family match. If Matthew relapsed and needed a transplant, our doctors would search for an unrelated donor on the National Marrow Donor Program. Many leukemia patients need an unrelated donor. I've read that 70% of patients who need a transplant won't have a match in their family. Many lives have been saved or extended thanks to unrelated donors. There are over 10.5 million registered as potential donors. If it was determined that my marrow was the best match for a desperate patient, whether they lived in Chicago or India, I would give my marrow in a heartbeat. What a gift to give hope to one who has run out of hope, just as our hope was renewed that very special clinic day. Davis was on his way to a bone marrow transplant.

## Chapter 8

# Fear Not, I Will

*Fear not, for I am with you;*
*be not dismayed, for I am your God;*
*I will strengthen you, I will help you,*
*I will uphold you with my righteous hand.*
**Isaiah 41:10**

*I will not leave you or forsake you.*
**Joshua 1:5**

Cancer involves the whole family, with each member facing particular challenges. In our family, I observed how deeply leukemia affected even our two healthy children, Elise and Bradley. Thankfully, Elise was so young when the boys were diagnosed that, developmentally, her little mind and emotions were shielded from much of the chaos the rest of us experienced. Even

*Our Help*

though it was unsettling for her to be shuffled around and separated from Mommy, she adapted well to the changes in her toddler world. For the most part, she was unaware of the weight or seriousness of our situation. Unfortunately, this was not the case for Bradley, our oldest child, our keenly observant son. To my dismay, Bradley saw cancer up close. Through his six-year-old-and-beyond eyes, he saw what it did to his brothers, his sister, his mom and dad. He also saw and experienced what leukemia did to him.

The first sting of being a sibling of a child with cancer is Mom and Dad's absence. Since Bradley was used to having me home all day, my absence was a deep shift in his world. Our wonderful friend, Hanna, who has cleaned our house regularly all these years, told me how hard it was for her to watch young Bradley come home from school during those months when most of my days were spent at the clinic or hospital. When he walked into the house through the garage door, he would immediately scan the kitchen in hope of seeing me. If he didn't, he would call out my name, hoping to hear my response. When silence followed, and he realized I wasn't home, Hanna watched his entire face droop. Bradley came home to Tara, but as nice as she was, she wasn't Mom. He wanted me. When I was home, I squeezed in as much fun "mom-time" as I could with Bradley. I wanted him to have his normal life, but many times

*Fear Not, I Will*

I could not shelter him from the reality of our situation. Life, as we knew it, wasn't normal anymore. Bradley knew our home and family life were now serious, scary, and different. The stability he'd had before had drastically changed.

The special attention Matthew and Davis received was also overwhelming. People were so thoughtful, supportive, and kind. But all this attention was hard to watch through a sibling's eyes. Every time someone stopped by to see us, either at home or at the hospital, they brought a gift for our boys fighting cancer. This selective generosity caused conflicting feelings for Bradley. He wasn't upset that Matthew and Davis were getting gifts, but it challenged his own value in our family in ways he could not describe. To him, it must have felt like a Christmas Day when his brothers got gifts—but he did not. I was always appreciative of the friend or family member who brought along a special gift for both Bradley and Elise as well. A general family gift was best. Davis and Matthew even got presents from the nurses. A trip to the treasure chest was a pleasant way to end a day at the clinic that had involved check-ups, "pokes," and chemo, but we started to notice Bradley felt slighted. We began to monitor the gifts coming home, at times asking Matthew if he would pick out a toy or game for his older brother. The special gifts and attention were never meant to purposely exclude Bradley, but I noticed my happy boy was becoming quiet and reserved when the focus was on Matthew and Davis.

By late fall of 1994, Bradley noticed another sibling getting tons of attention: his sister, Elise. She was the "perfect match" for Davis and, of course, since this was incredible, wonderful news, there was a lot of discussion with family and friends about her role in our fight with leukemia. After the transplant, people would sometimes refer to Elise as a brave hero. I understand why people described her in this way, and we are delighted she played that role for Davis, but then again, it wasn't entirely accurate. She didn't know what bone marrow was or what that meant for her little brother. She was too young to make any personal decision to save her brother's life. (Although, if she had been older, we know she would have agreed to it wholeheartedly!)

Not only were Matthew and Davis getting mounds of attention, but now Elise was being praised and treated as a hero. A real, understandable feeling of neglect was growing in Bradley, and he had to deal with these sad, confusing feelings primarily on his own. It was uniquely his pain. I wasn't fully aware of his struggles at the time, but I had sensed some of it, and it concerned me. Many times when I headed off to the hospital or clinic, I would pray specifically for my dear Bradley. "God, let him know I love him even though I can't be with him today. Surround him with my love and Yours."

Studies show that siblings of children with cancer experience their own trauma. Brothers or sisters of a child with cancer (or two, in our case) deal with multiple emotions. One study surveyed 30 siblings of childhood cancer. It listed the many different emotions described by this group: fear, anxiety, confusion, resentment, anger, jealousy, guilt, loneliness, isolation, and feelings of insecurity. Most expressed and experienced enduring sadness that lingered years after the crisis was over. One sibling in the survey summed up the whole experience like this: "Cancer is very painful inside. Very sad." But the predominant feeling expressed by all interviewed was the feeling of loss.

The study divided the loss into two categories. The first is the loss of the family's way of life. Bradley's life looked a lot different after the boys were diagnosed. Home life was unpredictable and unsettling. Bradley was home with his little sister, but beyond that, the rest of us came and went. He missed playing with his brothers, especially Matthew, since they were so close in age. He didn't like going to bed alone, without Matthew—they had shared a room since Matthew was born. He was sad his brothers were so sick and so often in the hospital; their loss of health was a loss for him as well. I rarely made his favorite foods anymore, and we rarely went to church together. So much had changed for Bradley, and he knew it wasn't good.

*Our Help*

The second category of loss is the loss of self within the family. Bradley didn't have leukemia; he wasn't the parent; and he wasn't the sibling marrow donor. In the years that followed, Wes and I were often asked to share our leukemia story at our church and other churches. We should have been more sensitive of the effect this had on Bradley. We often focused on the details of Davis' and Matthew's diagnoses and drew special attention to Elise's role in the transplant. As Bradley sat in the front row listening to us, he must have asked himself this question: "Where's *my* place in this story?" When I began to understand this, it crushed me to think Bradley wrestled with a diminished sense of self in this family story. He suppressed these insecure feelings and never made a fuss, but I noticed he would withdraw and leave the room when the subject of leukemia came up—and it came up many times. Both Bradley's brothers were granted Make-A-Wishes. We all enjoyed going to Disney World (Matthew's wish) and the Jumpin' Jamboree trampoline party (Davis'), yet these wonderful wishes were still his brothers' wishes, not his. (By the way, the next time the media shares a big story on a child whose wish is extravagantly granted, like being Batman-for-a-day or meeting a celebrity or professional athlete, celebrate the goodness of people but also think and pray for the siblings involved. The grand, singled-out attention can be potentially confusing and hard for them.)

Bradley also had to deal with media attention that was focused solely on Matthew and Davis. Many newspaper articles were written about their ordeal. One popular publication ran a two-day, front-page story. Another article was about a Glen Ellyn community fundraiser organized by a very thoughtful and energetic friend, Carol Van Gorp. We were deeply appreciative of all who joined us that fun night and generously contributed (the funds raised gave us the ability to pay off medical expenses our insurance did not pick up). Unfortunately, though, the publicity and public attention made Bradley feel even more excluded.

Almost 12 years after Davis' and Matthew's diagnoses, the Leukemia Research Foundation asked if our story could be featured on TV during Channel 7's coverage of the annual Jim Gibbons Run. Jim Gibbons was an anchorman who'd died years before from leukemia. The popular run raised funds for continued research into cures for leukemia and other blood diseases. I agreed to do the interview, which would be filmed in our home. That morning, before Brad, then a high school senior, headed off to school, I told him what I was doing that day. I downplayed the whole thing but wanted him to know that if he arrived home from track practice early, Channel 7 news trucks might be in the driveway. He shouldn't worry; nothing was wrong. I was simply being interviewed. I thought that was the end of it.

*Our Help*

That afternoon, the camera crew came in and within minutes transformed our family room into a TV studio. They rearranged furniture and set up extra light sources. The director made certain every detail was perfect for filming. The interview was going smoothly until we heard a disruption coming from the laundry room. It sounded like someone was entering through the garage door, but no one was expected home at that time. The younger two kids were still in school, and Matt and Brad were at track practice. Suddenly, a group of high school track athletes entered the family room. Leading the pack was Brad.

Before I could speak, the director immediately and firmly told them to leave. My dear son replied, "You can't tell me to leave; this is my house." Brad's response only made the director more determined to kick them out. My eyes met Brad's. "Please, Brad, this is almost over. Let me finish. You and the guys need to head out." I wasn't mad at him; yet I was taken aback at Brad's rebellion toward the director. He'd purposefully interrupted this interview, and he'd brought his friends to help him out. Brad obliged me, though he made his feelings clear. "Come on, guys," he said with an edge in his voice. "Let's get out of here."

The interview continued. The camera was rolling and I was talking when we again heard a commotion. This time it came from the backyard, directly behind me. Brad and his friends had formed a circle and were

*Fear Not, I Will*

playing catch, intentionally talking loudly enough to be heard through the window. The director again called, "Cut!" and angrily headed toward the back door. I stopped him and looked at everyone. I wanted to explain Brad's behavior. I knew this out-of-the-norm rebellion was a direct result of a far deeper issue. In that moment, I wished I had never agreed to the interview.

I didn't have to say much. One of the people in the room was a kind, thoughtful man from the Leukemia Research Foundation who understood the psychological effects Brad was experiencing as the sibling of two children with cancer. He was also sympathetic to him. He spoke up, giving the film crew a quick yet accurate reason for Brad's behavior. He then volunteered to talk to Brad and his friends. The director agreed, and my new friend went out on the back deck to talk with Brad. In a matter of moments, Brad and his gang headed back to school to finish track practice.

After the interview was finished, I left to pick up Brad from practice. I wasn't mad at him, but I did feel we needed to talk. When I drove up to the school, I noticed Brad was with a friend. Brad got into the front seat and quickly asked if we could give his friend a ride home. "Nice buffer," I thought. I turned to the young man as he was getting in the back seat and noticed he, too, had been at my house earlier that afternoon. Brad looked a bit sheepish and offered up a genuine apology. (I love

*Our Help*

this about Brad—he is always so quick to make things right.) I could tell he was wondering if I was going to punish him. I assured him I understood—or at least I thought I understood. I felt I should shed some light on the situation for Brad's friend, so I glanced back at him and said, "During our family crisis with leukemia, Brad felt left out." And then it happened. Twelve years post cancer crisis, the truth came out. Brad corrected me immediately. With anger in his tone, he emphatically set the record straight: "Felt left out, Mom? I *was* left out."

The hurt in his words was as palpable as the anger. This was the first time I'd heard Brad clearly express what happened to him when leukemia showed up at our house. As painful as it was to hear those words, I was relieved he had finally said them out loud and he'd said them directly to me. I was proud of him for getting it out. It gave Wes and me the opportunity to sit down that evening and discuss the topic with him, just him. We listened and asked him questions. We did our best to communicate that we understood. We assured him how significant he was and always will be in our family. Though leukemia deeply affected our family life, it did not define us as a family. It was not our whole story, just a chapter. We suggested a therapist who could help Brad with these emotions. We were ready and willing to do anything to help our son work through the deep-seated resentment and sadness he had felt all these years.

He'd experienced a major loss throughout his childhood; maybe now was the time to address it head on.

Brad assured us he was gaining a better perspective now that he was older, and he thought that as time went on, he would continue to have a clearer understanding of how leukemia changed each one of us in the family. While he still felt the sting of insignificance within this story, he understood why people wanted to hear about his brothers. As I listened to him talk, I realized I would never fully grasp what leukemia did to our son, Brad. I would never know its full impact on him. That night, Wes and I admired how openly Brad communicated and expressed his feelings. We told him how much we loved him and how proud we were of him. As we continued talking around the kitchen table that evening, I had the sense that an old heartache, finally revealed, was beginning to heal.

Children who have battled through cancer and are cured are called childhood cancer survivors. Brad is a childhood cancer survivor as well. Leukemia may not have attacked his body, but it certainly invaded his heart. He, too, needed help. "Our help is in the name of the Lord, who made heaven and earth" rang true for Brad just as much as it did for anyone in our family. In the midst of Brad's unique uncertainty and loss, God was always faithful.

Under God's care, Brad was never left out.

## Chapter 9

# Comfort in Affliction

*Blessed be the God and Father of our Lord Jesus Christ, the Father of mercies and God of all comfort, who comforts us in all our affliction, so that we may be able to comfort those who are in any affliction, with the comfort with which we ourselves are comforted by God.*
**2 Corinthians 1:3-4**

Davis still needed quite a bit of treatment before he was ready for a bone marrow transplant. Dr. Hayani's plan was to keep Davis on his original chemotherapy protocol until everything was set for his transplant. Davis' protocol called for extremely high doses of chemo, doses that far exceeded the amount any adult could endure. Dr. Hayani explained the reason: because Davis' organs were so new and young, he could actually withstand these high doses, and he desperately needed them; lesser amounts would not have bought us enough time. We were racing against time, hoping we could get Davis to transplant before he relapsed. Trying to prepare us for the worst, the doctors told us Davis could die at any time during treatment for three main reasons: the disease itself; organ failure due to the extremely high doses of chemo; or an infection his body couldn't fight off due to his weakened immune system. We hated the reality of this lopsided battle between a very powerful disease and Davis' frail body, but God continued to sustain him.

During the two-month wait, Davis was often hospitalized, sometimes to administer chemo, other times to treat an infection. Matthew was also admitted a few times because he had a fever, a central line infection, or a different complication related to his treatment. When the boys were admitted, they stayed for a minimum of three days. During these many visits we got to know other families who had a child with cancer. The first family we met (when Matthew was in for the initial diagnosis) was the Ball family. Dave and Linda had a third-grade son, Jeff, who, like Matthew, had been diagnosed with leukemia. Linda was pregnant with her fourth at that time—cancer rarely comes when convenient. The Balls were dealing with many of the same medical concerns we had, and we formed an instant bond. They knew and understood. The fears, the chemo, the heartache of watching your child in pain—they got it. We were not

*Comfort in Affliction*

alone in our suffering. We would often talk out in the hospital hallway, supporting each other as best we could. Some days our conversations were more serious than others, but there were other days we could simply enjoy their company, encourage one another, and laugh.

Surprisingly, laughter found its place in this whole, awful experience. There was still joy in the midst of pain, real, genuine joy. This trial did not stop Wes and me from seeing the humor in the little things of life—even if we did have two kids with stupid cancer. To be honest, I depended on Wes' humor. This personality trait in my husband was a godsend; it diffused a lot of the day-to-day stress. One of the reasons I survived those dark days was because of Wes. He made me smile, laugh, and see the joy in life even when my heart was breaking. Other families, doctors, and nurses appreciated his quick wit as well. People smiled when Wes was around. His sincere concern, accompanied with appropriate humor, was the right mix for families dealing with heartache on the pediatric floor.

That fall I also met a family who had a toddler girl with leukemia. I spotted her in the hallway and was drawn to her immediately. Her name was Beth—great name! She was so cute as she shuffled around in her pink, fuzzy robe and matching slippers. Her mom walked beside her, pushing Beth's IV pole. I introduced myself to the mom. Barb told me she had heard of us and was

*Our Help*

hoping we'd meet. As we talked, I learned little Beth had had a bone marrow transplant seven months before at one of the hospitals we were considering, Children's Hospital of Wisconsin in Milwaukee. Barb shared with me a little about the hospital and what I should expect. I began to get a sense of how difficult this was going to be for Davis and our family.

As Barb shared her story, I understood that part of the trauma for her was watching—and getting to know and care about—other families with very sick children. She'd known many who died while she was there. I didn't want to think about this; it reminded me how easily leukemia could take either of my boys, and even if they made it, through their cancer journeys I would know others who didn't, and my heart would be broken over and over. I felt fear set in again, along with a deeper understanding about our own, personal fight for life. The reality is leukemia kills, even very sweet, young children, even innocent babies. Little Beth continued to do well for another year but then relapsed the following fall. She passed away in the spring of 1996. I will never forget that sweet, chubby-cheeked girl wearing the pink robe and slippers. Leukemia never gave her a chance to be a healthy little girl or grow up to be a young lady. My heart still grieves for her family.

We also spent a lot of time, both in clinic and in the hospital, with Jim, Dottie, and Michael. Michael had lymphoma. He was about a year or two older than Matthew, and the two often played games together at the clinic. One day Michael developed serious side effects from the chemo and had to be hospitalized. He was placed in the intensive care unit. Davis was also in the hospital at that time, and his room was just one door down from Michael's.

Davis had been admitted to start a series of chemotherapy stays. This first visit would last a week to ten days, long enough for him to receive—and recover from—a huge bag of methotrexate. This bag of yellow fluid was nicknamed "liquid gold" by the nurses because one bag alone was worth 10,000 dollars. Administered through an IV, the liquid gold dripped through Davis' central line over a 24-hour period. It was super strong, almost too strong. It had the potential to cause major organ damage and other serious side effects. If this chemo remained in his body, it could kill him. Thankfully there was another medicine called "The Rescue" that counteracted this threat. Basically, from what we understood, the chemo was to go in hard, get the job done, kill all fast-growing cells, and then get out of there as quickly as possible. The "rescue" medicine helped the chemo clear out quickly before causing major organ damage. It was a great plan—yet it was extremely hard on Davis. The main side effect was mouth sores—horrible, painful mouth sores. Davis stopped eating and drinking for days. He depended on

*Our Help*

the nutrition that was pushed through his IV to keep his weight up. Eventually, though, he would need to eat and drink on his own before they would release him to go home. His blood levels and liver enzymes also had to be normal.

With all these concerns, Davis had to be closely monitored, and the seriousness of his treatment was probably why we were strategically placed in the hospital room right next to pediatric ICU, one door away from our new friends, Jim and Dottie, and their very sick boy, Michael.

Michael was at a point in his treatment when everything seemed to be going wrong. Both Dottie and Jim tried to be strong, but at times the stress was too much. I remember spotting Jim in the parking lot one day. I caught up to him to find out how Michael's day had gone. He rolled down the window, looked at me, put his head in his hands, and began to sob. Finally the words came out, "I don't know what's going to happen to him. He's so sick. I'm so scared he won't make it." My heart ached for this man and his family. They knew what this disease might do to their son.

The next day, while Davis was taking a nap in his hospital room, I went next door to PICU to see Michael. He was in bad shape. He didn't even look like a child. My mind flashed back to my dad as he battled his lymphoma. Even though Michael was awake, he could not respond to me. He just stared off in space. I tried to say something encouraging to Dottie and Jim, but that didn't go well. My words were hollow and flat. So, I stopped talking and listened. I listened to how Michael was diagnosed with lymphoma and the complications that led to this hospital stay and anything else they were willing to share. God was teaching me to listen, really listen. I needed to let other people tell their stories, to ask them questions, to sympathize with them when they expressed fear, anger, and stress. When I listened, I had a better sense of when to speak and what to say. It was not my job to fix it or to say just the right thing. My part was to communicate, in whatever way, that I cared. I was thankful I could support them in their journey with Michael.

Another sad but poignant encounter happened when I was in the nurses' lounge heating up Davis' baby food. While waiting for the microwave to beep, I usually read the nurse's bulletin board or looked in the fridge to see what the nurses were eating (pretty unhealthy stuff!), but today there was a woman sitting at the table tape-recording Bible verses. This intrigued me, so I smiled at her, which caused her to turn off the tape-recorder and look at me. "The Bible is very comforting during difficult times, isn't it?" I said as an introduction. That opened the door just enough for her to share her story. Her teenage son had been terribly burned in a house fire. He wasn't

*Our Help*

expected to live much longer. His major organs were failing. She wanted to comfort and help him transition from this life to life in heaven, so she had the idea of taping verses and playing them over and over, close to his ear, throughout the night. She said he was not conscious, but she hoped he would hear God's words of love and peace while he exited this world and met God face to face. She expressed a strong, personal love for God.

She then asked why I was at Loyola. I gave a short answer about Davis and Matthew, and she said she would pray for my boys. Right then. She reached out her hand for mine and began praying. We sat in the nurses' lounge and prayed for *our* boys. It was an unexpected, sacred moment I will cherish the rest of my life. She was about to lose her son, and she was praying for mine. Her son died in the middle of the night, listening to his mother's tape-recorder, hearing the words of God. I can't imagine what those following days and weeks were like for her, but I do know she depended on God for strength and trusted Him with her son's life and death. She was a beautiful example to me of how I could respond when faced with such sorrow, of how I could still minister to others even when going through deep, personal pain. What a godly, gracious, and wise mom. I'm so thankful our paths crossed.

## Chapter 10

# Take Refuge

*The Lord is good,
a stronghold in the day of trouble;
he knows those who take refuge in him.*
**Nahum 1:7**

It took another ten-day hospital stay for Davis to receive his second bag of liquid gold, but finally, on a Friday in mid-December, we were all home together. Wes and I had the joy of putting all four of our kids to bed that night. In the past three months, this routine activity had rarely happened, but we were thrilled when it did. In fact, we were looking forward to being home most of the week, since Christmas was a week away and the clinic was closed. The timing was good because we were also in the process of selling our house, and the realtor was coming by with a prospective buyer the very next morning after we arrived home. As Wes would say, "We didn't think we had enough stress, so we thought we'd sell our house!" There's that humor I had grown to love.

We were selling our house because Wes and I were afraid it was a potential environmental threat to our children's health. What if something in our house caused the leukemia? The thought scared me. Maybe we were panicking or over-reacting, but even if we were, we felt we had to get out of that house. My brother, Dave, and my sister-in-law, Jean, supported our decision, and Jean took it upon herself to find us a new house. Knowing Jean, I was sure she would get the job done quickly. Within a few weeks, she found a lot on the north side of the tracks, close to our little downtown, where a new house was being built. It sounded perfect, and we ended up purchasing the home fairly quickly. The anticipation of living in a brand new home gave us something to look forward to, and we planned on moving into it in March, April, or whenever we were past the bone marrow transplant. *Everything* was on hold until after the transplant.

One weekend, Wes and I had a chance to drive by the lot. The frame of the house was up, allowing us to get an idea of the layout. To most new homeowners, this would be an exciting part of the process, but not to me. I had no interest in any of it. I never once looked at the blueprint. I didn't care how big the rooms were or how many bathrooms we had. I didn't pick tile or carpet. I didn't pick out the kitchen cabinets or fixtures. I didn't know if my laundry room was on the first floor or in the basement. I left all decisions to the builder. I really didn't care. All I cared about was to someday look out my back kitchen window (if the house had one—I assumed it did) to see our four, healthy children playing in the backyard. Not two children, not three, but all four. That was all it would take for this to be my dream home.

As the prospective buyers walked through our house, Davis and I drove around in the car, listening to Christmas music (the rest of the family was at church). I glanced over at him and noticed his cheeks were flushed. Was it from the cold air I had exposed him to when we got in the car? I felt his forehead. He felt warm. Oh no! I knew what this meant. This meant a trip back to the hospital. Even though I was concerned about any fever Davis had, I have to admit I was disappointed too—we had a family party planned for that afternoon to celebrate Bradley's seventh birthday. Grandma, Nana and Papa, aunts, uncles, and cousins were coming over. This was to be Bradley's day. He was looking forward to his party, and the thought of canceling or missing it made my heart sink; he would be so disappointed. Once back at the house, I gave Davis some Tylenol and put him down for his nap. My hope was he would sleep through Bradley's party, and the fever would naturally

*Our Help*

return to normal. Maybe a call to Dr. Hayani would not be necessary.

Thankfully, Davis took a solid, three-hour nap, and we all celebrated Bradley's birthday. It worked out perfectly—sort of. After all the gifts were opened and the cake devoured, I quickly ran upstairs, woke Davis, and took his temp again: 102. It was time to call Dr. Hayani and return to the hospital. I walked downstairs and broke the concerning news to Wes. He was disappointed, too. We were together as a family one full day. Just one. Wes had really wanted to stop by at a Christmas party to visit friends he hadn't seen for a long time, yet within an hour, he was on his way instead to Loyola with Davis. I stayed home with the others. Two days later we had another surprise: Matthew woke up with a fever! Within a few hours, he and I were on our way to join Davis and Wes. As I walked into a double room set up specifically for both our boys, my eyes met Wes' and we smiled at each other. This was bound to happen, but at least we were in it together.

The reason for both fevers was unknown; the doctors thought they were caused by an infection from their central lines. No matter what the reason was, Davis and Matthew had to stay in the hospital for three to five days while the doctors watched their blood cultures for bacteria. Since we were only a few days away from Christmas, I worried, wondering if we would be home

*Take Refuge*

in time. Wes and I began to creatively plan how we could celebrate Christmas in the boys' hospital room if we needed to. We decided we would bring in an artificial tree, decorations, stockings, and presents. It wouldn't be ideal, but we could make it work. It might even be a fun adventure, one the kids would never forget. We would have to wait and see. Bradley was off school that week, so on one of the days, Wes dropped him off at the hospital in the morning and he stayed the entire day. What a treat for his brothers! Matthew loved Bradley's company. They played video games, ate a "hospital" lunch, and watched more TV than ever allowed at home. In the afternoon, while Davis and Matthew took a nap, Bradley and I played a game of Guess Who on the floor in the hallway. Bradley had a new perspective and a better understanding regarding Matthew's and Davis' hospital days. In some small way, I hoped this enjoyable day calmed his fears. I wasn't going to tell him not all days were like that happy one.

The next day, a radiologist I had never before met walked in and asked to speak with me. He had results back from one of Davis' CAT scans. He told me they'd found spots on Davis' liver and spleen. This could indicate a number of things, he said, including cancerous tumors. This news sent a shock wave through my body. If this was true, the BMT was off. Had I just been told it was over, that hope was gone? I forced myself to be strong

*Our Help*

and calm in front of my boys. I asked the nurse to send Dr. Hayani to our room as soon as he came to the floor to make his rounds. He arrived shortly after, and I gave him the radiologist's report. He had already reviewed the film and quickly assured me he did not believe it was cancer but rather an infection that could be treated with an aggressive antibiotic and anti-fungal medication. He had seen this before and was not alarmed. He grabbed hold of my arm, looked me in the eye, and calmly said, "It's going to be all right, Beth. This setback will not delay Davis' bone marrow transplant."

As soon as I heard, "all right," I exhaled. Then the tears started to flow out of sheer relief. Dr. Hayani sat down next to Matthew in his bed and assured him *Mommy* was going to be all right. Happy tears are still tears to a little boy, though, so I appreciated Dr. Hayani reassuring him while I regained my composure. The bone marrow transplant was still a go.

Matthew's temperature had been normal for two days, and his blood cultures were not showing any bacteria growth, so Dr. Hayani scheduled him to be discharged the next day. Davis, however, needed to stay at least a day or two longer for one more CAT scan and other tests in preparation for his BMT. Matthew was, of course, glad to head home, but this had been a good hospital visit for him. The main reason: Matthew loved hospital scrambled eggs with melted cheese on top.

*Take Refuge*

Seriously, he went crazy over Loyola's signature cheesy eggs! Whenever we made scrambled eggs at home from that point on, cheese on top was a must. Davis was going to miss his roommate, and, no doubt, Matthew was going to miss the yummy, cheesy eggs.

The next night, while getting Davis ready for bed, I noticed a commotion out in the hallway. I knew this meant a crisis for another family. I could sense the tension and stress, the quiet disbelief and fear. I could, with pretty good accuracy, pick out who was who in the group. Mom and dad were sitting in the family crisis room with extended family around them. Their pastor was at the doorway of this room monitoring the flow of church members and friends. I watched them all, studied their faces. Once Davis was settled in for the night and asleep, I went out in the hall for a minute and made contact with one of the somber friends. "How can I pray for you?" I asked. The heartache was revealed: a young brother and sister were riding home on I-290 with their grandmother when a semi-truck hit them. The grandmother was in serious but stable condition and being treated on a different floor, but her grandchildren were in critical condition. The boy's situation was grave.

Everyone was so quiet. One could feel the heartache and sorrow that filled the hallway that night. I finally closed my door. In the morning, I immediately checked

*Our Help*

the situation. The boy hadn't died, but it wasn't looking good. Family, friends, and church members poured in all day, surrounding the parents with love and prayers. It was beautiful to watch. In the midst of their great pain, they were blessed with a loving, supportive community. God was helping them just as He had helped us when our crisis began.

That morning, Christmas Eve day, I received good news: Davis and I were going home for Christmas! I called Wes and then began gathering all my things, signing release papers, getting instructions from the nurses, and making multiple trips down to the car. As I returned from one trip, Dr. Hayani flagged me down in the hallway. He had bad news. He'd just gotten a call from the lab: Matthew's blood cultures showed bacteria growth. This required Matthew to return to the hospital for another five days of antibiotics. The awful, sick feeling returned, but Dr. Hayani put me at ease immediately. "Don't worry, I have a plan. I want you all home for Christmas." He would never risk our boys' health, but when it was safe to go against protocol for the sake of some valuable family time, Dr. Hayani was always supportive. Home health care would teach Wes and me how to administer the antibiotics through a portable IV the boys would wear inside a little fanny pack. It sounded complicated (and it was), but I was willing to do whatever it took to be home. I put Davis' cute hat and coat on, picked him up, and walked out of the hospital. We were heading home for Christmas.

(This was not the case for that dear family with the two children who'd been in a car accident. We later found out the young boy died the day we left the hospital, Christmas Eve. His sister died a week later. *Oh Lord, we lean on You when our hearts and minds are full of questions. Help us to trust You in the midst of such uncertainty and grief. Give us the intense awareness that today is a gift, and we should not take it for granted. No one is guaranteed a tomorrow on this earth. Help this family and help me with this truth.*)

## Chapter 11

# Prayers of Many

*On him we have set our hope that
he will deliver us again.
You also must help us by prayer, so that many
will give thanks on our behalf for the blessings
granted us through the prayers of many.*
**2 Corinthians 1:10-11**

Every moment was cherished on Christmas Day. The Christmas shopping I had done that past summer prior to diagnosis turned out to be the best decision—I had zero time to shop in December. On Christmas morning, Bradley and Matthew screamed for joy when they got the latest, popular Power Ranger toy action figures. Elise's eyes widened as she realized the super-big box was hers to open. A Little Tikes kitchen had arrived just in time for her to make a pretend breakfast for all of us (a sign of things to come). Davis even entered into the fun, though not for very long since his energy was low.

Davis was rail thin and weak due to the intense chemo rounds he'd had over the past few weeks. He seemed to have just enough energy to play with the bow that had once decorated his gift. I held him in my arms for most of the day. *Is this our last Christmas together?* I couldn't stop this sickening thought from haunting me. What would this year bring for Davis, Matthew, for our whole family? The significance of this day was also difficult for Wes. I saw his eyes fill with tears more than once as he watched the kids play with their new toys. We did our best to shield these emotions from the children. They were not burdened with future possibilities, and we tried to do the same. That evening we went over to my mom's place for dinner. The table was beautifully set and the meal was truly "comfort" food. I loved being in her home...I loved being with my mom. As we sat around her table, my heart was filled with thankfulness. We had a wonderful Christmas. What a gift!

Another gift was getting to meet my new baby niece, Marissa. My brother Paul and sister-in-law Deborah had just welcomed this little cutie into their home, and we got to meet her when we had our family Christmas gathering. What joy her little life brought to our family. She and Davis were only six months apart, and I knew they would become close. *Cousins for life*,

I prayed, and I imagined their friendship stretching through their childhood years and into their teens. Again I immersed myself in the joy of the present. This helped me push away thoughts of Davis' bone marrow transplant, thoughts that were never far from my mind.

January 3, 1995, the day before we headed to Milwaukee for Davis' transplant, was packed with activity. Every minute was full, yet in the middle of this busyness, God placed moments of incredible significance. It is a day I will never forget. In the morning we went to the Cancer Treatment Center with Matthew and Davis, who both had to be in the clinic. Davis got a checkup and a sweet good-bye hug from Dr. Hayani. Dr. Hayani was now handing Davis' medical care over to the transplant doctor at the Children's Hospital of Wisconsin (CHW). Matthew also had a check up and then a round of chemo in the early afternoon. We got home just in time for a *Chicago Tribune* interview; the newspaper was running a story about our boys' leukemia and the upcoming transplant. Right after the interview, the same couple who'd looked at our house the Sunday before Christmas came back, with their realtor, to look at the house one more time. While they were walking through the house, a friend stopped by to drop off a meal. It was a special dinner; we were celebrating two birthdays early, Matthew's and Elise's, since we would not all be home when they turned five

*Our Help*

and three. In the middle of all this, I somehow found time to pack for both Davis and myself. Davis could potentially be in the hospital for two or three months. We had no idea how long it would take. Even as I packed all we would need for an extended stay, I tried not to think about this.

Dinnertime was extremely overwhelming and busy. The kids were excited to celebrate two birthdays, yet Wes and I felt the weight and significance of this moment. We took pictures and even some video. We were doing our best to be upbeat and happy in front of the kids, but inwardly we both were struggling. We had no idea when we would be together again.

After we sang the last "Happy Birthday" and started eating our cake, Wes and I heard a noise outside. It wasn't the normal sound of cars going by our house. It sounded like footsteps. Did I hear people talking? We headed to the window to see what was going on. Nothing should be going on outside; no one should be out there because it was bitterly, bitterly cold. The weatherman had predicted record-low temperatures, well below zero by early evening. When I leaned near the window to look outside, I could feel the cold on my face. But then I could also see—and it was an image I will treasure for the rest of my life. I couldn't believe my eyes at first; people were gathering in front of our house. Then they started to form a circle. More and more people came, walking up the sidewalk or running across the street to join those already in our yard. Then I noticed children, bundled up tightly so only their eyes were exposed to the wicked cold. The circle of people soon extended around our entire house. At first I couldn't figure it all out. What were they doing? Then we heard them. They began singing and then small groups within the circle started praying. They were there to pray for us and sing praises to God, the One who would help us. It was the most beautiful sight and sound.

Wes, Bradley, Matthew, Elise, and I stood at the front window speechless. I held Davis in my arms and felt them holding me up in the same way through their prayers. All those dear people braved the frigid cold to intercede on our behalf, to plead with God to bring Davis back home healthy and well, to pray for healing and protection for Matthew and protection for Bradley and Elise, too. I was overwhelmed by the support from our church family and neighbors that cold, cold night. What love! My weary soul was strengthened and my hope restored. Their faith gave us faith. There was no doubt in my mind, after witnessing this display of love, that God would be with us every step of the way.

Morning came. It was time to leave for Milwaukee. I fought back the tears as I said goodbye to Bradley, Matthew, and Elise. I was so thankful for Tara. She kept the rhythm of the house going. She knew the kids'

*Our Help*

schedules and would stay with them at night while both Wes and I were gone. But I still didn't want to say goodbye. I knew I would not see Elise until right before the transplant, which was scheduled for January 13, over a week away. I would not see Bradley and Matthew for even longer. Matthew would turn five, Elise would turn three, and I would not be there on those special days. Bradley needed me. Elise needed me. And Matthew—how could I leave him? He had leukemia. What mother or father leaves the state when their five-year-old son has leukemia? Unthinkable.

A verse from Hebrews 12 encouraged me the most during that time. It read, "And let us run with perseverance the race marked out for us, fixing our eyes on Jesus, the author and perfecter of our faith." This part of my "life race" was tough, and my endurance was challenged. But I knew if I fixed my eyes on Jesus, I would persevere. God was my focal point. He was my Sustainer. He enabled me to put one foot in front of the other, guiding me when I didn't know where I was going or where my family was headed. No matter what, I wanted God's plan and God's purpose for my children. In the uncertainty of our future, I once again had to surrender my doubts and fears to my Lord and Savior, my divine Help, the Maker of heaven and earth.

He was my help that very morning, giving me the strength I needed to hug and kiss Bradley, Matthew, and

*Prayers of Many*

Elise and head north for Wisconsin, on a new journey with Davis that would forever alter our lives.

Two hours later we were in Milwaukee, pulling into the parking lot at the massive Children's Hospital of Wisconsin. We went directly to the pediatric oncology clinic. Our new hematology and transplant doctor, Dr. Casper, met with us for a few minutes while the nurses started an IV for Davis. Before heading to his room, we were handed a huge stack of papers that explained the bone marrow transplant and all its possible risks. Each risk was accompanied with a box or line for us to initial or sign, showing we understood the danger and gave our consent for the treatment. The huge stack was not only intimidating, it was frightening. Wes and I knew the transplant was our only medical option for Davis' survival, yet it was so hard to acknowledge that our signatures and agreement to treatment put Davis in great danger. The extremely high doses of chemotherapy drugs could cause significant damage to his internal organs or even death. Our consent to radiation could significantly damage Davis' brain and other vital organs, and radiation at his age would cause serious growth issues. When he received the BMT, his body could reject the new marrow and battle a common yet deadly disease called graft vs. host disease. Another concern: since his body would have no—zero—blood counts for many days, the smallest infection or virus could take his life—instantly.

*Our Help*

Each time we signed our consent to one of these terrible risks, everything in me shouted, "NO!" I couldn't put my baby in such horrible danger! But the transplant gave Davis hope. We had no chance with chemotherapy. We knew children lived through a BMT and were cured, so we had to go forward with the transplant and trust God to care for Davis through it and beyond. I remembered the circle of praying people the night before. I remembered the elders of our church surrounding Davis, covering his little head with oil, and praying for his body to be healed. So many were praying. God had strategically assigned people around the world to pray for our family. We had to walk forward by faith. With tears in my eyes, I forced my way through all the consent forms, signing each line with a shaky hand and a fearful yet hopeful heart.

After all the consent forms were signed, we followed the nurse up to the HOT unit (Hematology, Oncology, and Transplant). We were given the room right next to the nurses' station, which brought me some comfort. Wes and I moved our stuff in and made it as cozy as we could. Like other families with a child in for a lengthy stay, we made the room look more like a child's bedroom than a sterile hospital one. We set up Davis' toys and rocker seat and then put away our clothes in the built-in drawers. I also set up a new CD player on the shelf. Davis loved to dance with his mommy or daddy, and we were not going to stop just because of the pending transplant. Dancing with Davis was a hospital highlight for me. I would start the music and dance over to Davis' hospital bed. My silly movements would get his attention and he'd start bouncing to the beat. He knew what was coming next. I swooped him up into my arms, grabbed the IV pole, and we danced around the room. Davis loved this! He would show a little grin, then a big smile, followed by the best belly laugh ever. Mission accomplished. The Proverb, "A joyful heart is good medicine," kept coming to mind as we danced our troubles away.

The first couple days on the HOT unit, Davis' blood counts were good, good enough to leave his room and discover our new surroundings. We took a lot of walks and introduced ourselves to wonderful nurses and families. It didn't take long for everyone to fall in love with Davis. He was so friendly. This new hospital didn't scare him; hospitals were like his second home. Surprisingly, Davis went from toddling to really walking while on this floor—on the very first day. The catheter and multiple IV lines protruding from his central line didn't stop him! Our skinny, 15-month-old Boy Wonder walked around the floor, mask over most of his face, pushing his little cart of blocks, and stopping at each door to wave "hi" to the other sick children resting in their beds. Then there was me, tagging along, pushing his IV pole, frantically trying to keep the lines from getting tangled or pulled.

*Our Help*

Like any proud parent, Wes videotaped his first real steps. We were both so glad he was there to witness this! Wes stayed for an extra day while I got settled in, and he then drove back to Glen Ellyn. He would return a week later with little Elise and her incredible gift of matching, healthy bone marrow.

One week before transplant (called Day 0) Davis received many different chemotherapy drugs. These high doses of chemo continued killing cancer cells and wiping out his marrow. Davis also had six rounds of radiation, starting two days before transplant. Radiation killed more cancer cells and was more effective than chemo at destroying Davis' cancer-making marrow. The goal was to wipe out all of it. We didn't want one cancer cell remaining. Radiation was done at a separate hospital attached to the Children's Hospital. We had to walk there twice a day for three days in a row. "The first trip is the hardest," the nurse warned me. She was right.

Using a special blue marker, the doctor drew lines all around Davis' major organs and had little plates tailor-made so they would cover and protect these areas when he was radiated. Davis and I were then ushered into a large, sterile room where I perched on a small stool and waited for the anesthesiologist. There we sat, Davis on my lap wearing only a diaper. I carefully studied Davis' baby toes, legs, hands, and blue-marked tummy. I kissed his little head that now had only a few wisps of hair.

*Prayers of Many*

He was too thin and the room was too cold. I looked around the room. There was no escape door. We had nowhere to go but through this awful experience. The anesthesiologist entered, picked up Davis' central line access, and pushed in the solution. Immediately, Davis went limp, collapsing in my arms. It was shocking and horrifying—he was out in a split second! I was asked to lay his limp, listless body on a long, thin cushion directly on the floor. The nurses began to position the organ plates and attach several wires to his small body. Davis' transplant nurse put her arm around me and led me out of the room.

The room she led me into looked like something out of a sci-fi movie, full of scary equipment. I noticed a video monitor that allowed me to see my baby while preparations continued. Nurses stretched his tiny arms to each side and spread apart his legs. They covered his eyes with small black patches, and then everyone left the room. Davis was alone. The technicians sat down at a huge, complicated, digital board. They were just about to get started when they noticed I was still there, staring at the scary equipment. One technician looked at me and then looked at the nurse. The nurse grabbed hold of my shoulders and guided me away from the view of my baby. She tried to take me to the waiting room, but I couldn't go there. I told her I needed to use the bathroom. She looked at me with sympathetic eyes and pointed me

*Our Help*

to a small, single bathroom. Once inside, I locked the door and tears came. My back slid down the wall, and I huddled on the floor grieving our decision. There was no turning back now. I had reached another new low. Davis would be forever changed due to the radiation that was invading his body at that very moment. "I'm so sorry, Davis, I'm so sorry," I whispered over and over.

## Chapter 12

# The One Who Helps

*Behold, God is my helper;*
*the Lord is the upholder of my life.*
**Psalm 54:4**

*For I, the Lord your God, hold your right hand;*
*it is I who say to you,*
*"Fear not, I am the One who helps you."*
**Isaiah 41:13**

On January 12, the day before transplant, Wes and Elise arrived. I was so happy to see them and wrapped my arms around my sweetie pie, Elise. I'd missed her so much. She had just turned three the day before, but she still looked so small to do something so big. She wasn't allowed to go into Davis' room, so she gave him a sweet wave from the window in the door.

*Our Help*

While the nurses watched Davis, Wes, Elise, and I had a quick dinner together in the cafeteria. Elise had to have one last pre-surgery blood draw at the clinic. Then she and I went to the Ronald McDonald house for the night while Wes stayed with Davis.

Elise loved the Ronald McDonald House. It was a fun, beautiful place. It had a big playroom, a video room (the older boys would enjoy this later), and great big stuffed animals to sit on while reading books. The room we stayed in resembled a hotel room and shared a bathroom with other rooms on that floor. Each floor also had a community kitchen for parents who had to stay at the Ronald McDonald House for months. I got Elise ready for bed, read her a story, and snuggled her in for the night. This time with my little girl was pure joy to me. I loved hearing her voice and being with her one-on-one. She, too, loved having a sleepover with Mommy. We were both in bed by 9 since we had to get up super early the next morning. We both slept well—it was a nice change from nights in the hospital room with nurses coming in and out every 30 minutes and IV machines continually buzzing and beeping. A good night's sleep is a beautiful thing, especially before a very important day.

Transplant Day had arrived. It was Friday the thirteenth. Without an ounce of superstition in me, I was excited and energized for the day. I awoke at 4:30, took a shower, got dressed, woke and dressed Elise, and we

*The One Who Helps*

were headed to the hospital by 5:45. Elise kept saying, "I'm hungry, Mommy." I knew she couldn't eat anything until after surgery, so I reminded her that after she was done helping Davis, she could eat whatever she wanted. She was content with that arrangement. It was precious to see her deep trust in me.

Elise took silly syrup to calm her fears (she told me I had two heads as we waited in the surgery holding room), and then the nurses wheeled her off to harvest her bone marrow. I kissed her gently and told her Daddy would be with her when she woke up, and she willingly went with them. It was hard for me to see her go, but I trusted God to protect her and keep her safe. While she was in surgery, Jeff and Lora arrived from Wheaton. What a blessing to have them join us on this very important day! After three long hours, Dr. Casper entered Davis' room to tell us he had harvested all the marrow he needed. The procedure was over and Elise was recovering well. Dr. Casper described the surgery: Elise had been poked in the back pelvic bone area eighty times. I gasped at the thought. Then he lifted his hand and showed us the quart-size bag of rich, thick, red marrow. I was shocked at how much they had taken from her, but this quickly changed to grateful amazement. This healthy marrow was for Davis. I was looking at the most gorgeous bag of marrow I would ever see. It had hope written all over it.

*Our Help*

Around 10 a.m. we were allowed to see Elise in the post-surgery room. Wes was the first to hold her. She was still fairly sedated but aware she was back in her daddy's safe arms. When it was my turn, I was careful not to press on the large, protective bandage that covered her back. I kissed her head and rubbed her cheek to comfort her. She had no idea how incredible this moment was to all her family, especially to her baby brother "Dabis."

Within an hour, Elise was in a room up on the HOT unit, just two doors down from Davis. Davis had received his last two rounds of radiation that day and was doing fairly well, but we could tell his appetite and energy were heading south fast. Elise was recovering well, eating grape popsicles and watching Winnie the Pooh. She enjoyed all the attention she was getting from her mom and dad and Jeff and Lora (who were like second parents to her). The only minor setback happened when Elise's hemoglobin started to drop. Dr. Casper gave orders for her to stay overnight in the hospital while her blood counts returned to normal.

After Elise fell asleep that evening, and Jeff and Lora said goodbye, Wes and I waited for the marrow to arrive back from the lab. All day, technicians had been cleaning and processing Elise's marrow so it was exactly the right "potion" for Davis. It seemed to take forever. Finally, close to midnight, the marrow was delivered to the HOT unit and given to the nurse. Papers were exchanged and signed, names were checked and double checked, and then the nurse brought a syringe filled with 20cc of "pure life" into Davis' hospital room. We all marveled at how different the marrow looked now. That huge bag of thick marrow had been processed down to a small amount, and it was not deep red anymore; it looked like watered-down red Gatorade. The nurse hooked the syringe up to Davis' IV machine, pulled up a chair, and sat there for the next hour. She was missile locked on the entire infusion process, making sure everything went according to plan. Wes and I also watched as the marrow flowed into the central line and then into Davis, who slept through the entire process, peacefully, without a worry in the world. He rested as restoration went to work.

Wes videotaped this critical and blessed moment. Afterwards, Wes set the video camera down, grabbed hold of my hand, and led me to the side of Davis' crib, where we quietly prayed over him. We prayed that the cancer would be gone, completely, forever gone. We prayed for Elise's marrow to graft. We prayed for protection from infections, complete healing, and a long, healthy life for Davis. We prayed for more faith to trust God's sovereignty. Davis was in God's hands, and we knew that was the best place for him to be.

By the next morning Elise's blood counts had returned to normal, and she was discharged. She waved

*Our Help*

goodbye to Davis and Daddy, and the two of us headed home. It was so good to reunite with Matthew and Bradley! Bradley told me everything that was going on in his little world. Matthew was feeling well because he had a week off chemo, and, thankfully, Elise's discomfort from the surgery was minimal. Her young, flexible bones contributed to her quick recovery. All she needed was a few doses of baby Tylenol, and she was good-to-go. The four of us had so much fun! The day after Elise and I got home, we stayed in the basement all day, just playing together. I was looking forward to being home the whole week.

On Wednesday evening, Wes called with some disturbing news. Wes had a slight sniffle, and Dr. Casper wanted him out of Davis' room ASAP. I had to switch places with him that very evening. There was no other option. Wes was terrified he might have exposed Davis to a virus. I was scared and worried, too. Davis could not come in contact with any bacteria or virus; it could kill him within days. I quickly packed my things while Wes' dear mom (our kids call her Nana) made her way over to stay with the other children. Wes' mom and dad lived about thirty minutes south of us and were always willing to help whenever we needed them. What a blessing to have extended family nearby.

Before leaving for Milwaukee, I had one more hard task: I had to break the news to Bradley, who was at

*The One Who Helps*

church that night, participating in AWANA. I drove over to the church and picked Bradley up earlier than he expected. He knew something was wrong right away. As we got into the elevator, I told him I had to leave. I told him the reason why, hoping he would understand. But Bradley was heartbroken. "You promised, Mom, you promised you'd stay with me!" he cried, hoping those words would change my mind. Big tears ran down his sweet face. The two of us went home, where I gathered my things and prepared to leave for Wisconsin. Bradley tried his best to hold on to me. He begged me to stay. I assured him I would be back as soon as possible. I didn't want to leave him so upset, but I knew I had to go—Davis' life was at risk. I loosened his grip on my arm, told him I loved him, and left. I prayed for my sad, discouraged son all the way to the Wisconsin border. Once I crossed the border, though, I changed my focus, bracing myself for the difficulty ahead. I was heading back into the cancer battle zone, where Davis was in the fight of his life.

Davis was much worse than when I'd left him. Wes had given me updates each day, but they hadn't prepared me for Davis' appearance. The trauma of the transplant was evident in his weakened body, and the radiation damage was also noticeable. Davis had awful mouth sores again; these indicated what was happening throughout his whole body. He was blistering and peeling from the

*Our Help*

inside out. I was horrified at this thought. He was unable to communicate the severity of his pain, but the nurses knew the signs and had put him on morphine for pain and lipids for nutrition. For a number of days, all Davis did was sleep, cry, moan, and stare off in space. When he slept, he had nightmares. To comfort him, I wrapped him in a blanket and rocked him for hours on end. Those days were long, so long, yet I was perfectly content sitting in the rocker, gently, quietly caring for my son. I knew his condition was critical. At night, when the room was dark and he was asleep, I would get out of bed and place my hands on his small, hairless head. As the six or more machines continued to keep my baby alive, I pleaded with God to protect and heal him. I was confident God understood how hard it was for me to watch my boy suffer. He had experienced this Himself with His own Son.

About ten days after transplant, Davis started to find interest in his toys again. As I was helping Davis play one day, I glanced up and saw—through the window in the door—a nurse running down the hallway towards our room. She had a huge smile on her face, and it was directed right at me. She taped a note on our door window. I quickly went over to read it: "Davis has counts—4!" Even though a healthy person has a blood count in the 1000s, our Davis had four, and the nurse and I were ecstatic! This was our first sign his new "Elise" marrow was grafting and producing normal, healthy blood cells. Amazing! I couldn't wait to tell Wes.

A few weeks before, my friend Melanie Rodemann shared our story with her mom, and her mom wanted to help. She graciously let us borrow a set of special phones to use while we were up at transplant, separated as a family. Each phone had a large viewing screen. I had one in Davis' hospital room; the other was in our kitchen back home. That evening I told Wes and the older kids the great news, and we had the best conversation. Since Wes and I were happy, the kids were happy. They pushed their little faces up to the screen, all wanting the closest view. They became sillier as we talked, and soon we were all laughing together. Davis even got in on the fun and pointed to each sibling with a little giggle. What a celebration those four cells gave us. This was just the news we needed to start hoping for the best.

## Chapter 13

# Consolation

*When I said, "My foot is slipping," your love, O* Lord, *supported me. When anxiety was great within me, your consolation brought joy to my soul.*
**Psalm 94:18-19**

The HOT unit was a hard place to be. Every child's situation was critical—far more serious than most of the patients' on Loyola's pediatric floor. Beth's mom, Barb, was right. Most rooms were dark, and parents were solemn. Sometimes a family member would be outside the room and want to talk. I soon found out which child was dying of AIDS, which teen was dying of lymphoma, and which toddler faced transplant that week. The patients were children—that's what made it so, so hard. Next door to our room was a teen who also had leukemia and a recent bone marrow transplant. He liked to listen

*Our Help*

to his music as loud as possible. Every day, I could feel the beat of the bass pounding through my wall. Then, one day, the music stopped, and family members, one after another, poured in and out of his room. Very early the next morning, I got up to check on Davis. Through the window in the door, I saw two men walk past. They were pushing a large, long box with a blanket draped over it. I stared as they slowly maneuvered the box into a staff-only elevator. I knew my teen neighbor was gone.

I hate leukemia. I hate death.

A day or two later, Davis got a fever. Fevers are critically serious for post-transplant patients. I could feel the anxiety the nurses and doctors were trying to hide from me. They covered it up with encouraging words, but they were all worried, and I knew it. Dr. Casper went home late that night and called the nurses' station hourly to get an update on Davis' fever. In the morning it was still there. This was not good. The tension grew. I tried not to let it get to me, but by late morning I was an emotional mess. I kept looking at the nurse, hoping to see a reassuring expression on her face, some indication that his fever was under control, but I got nothing. She had seen this all too often. A fever on the HOT unit can lead to death.

I called Wes and asked him to notify all our praying friends. We needed urgent, pleading prayers. I gathered Davis in my arms and began rocking him again.

I thought of the other parents on the floor who had lost a child. This couldn't be happening. A wave of fear and anxiety crashed over me. I tried to pray, but my mind was too worried. I kissed his little head over and over. There was nothing I could do for him. If an infection was in his body, he didn't have enough healthy cells to fight. He was much too weak and unarmed for this invasion. We had come so far. Was it really going to end this way?

I continued to rock Davis, trying to quiet my fearful thoughts—and failing. And then it happened again—God did what He had done so many times before. He comforted me with His truth, His perspective, His love. He sent my desperate thoughts of death in another direction—I started thinking about heaven. *"What's so wrong with heaven?"* I thought, *"To be with you, God, is far better than anything this world offers. If Davis dies, he will go from my arms directly to Yours. What a glorious healing he would experience. If You take him, I don't know what I'll do, but I know Davis will be wonderfully safe. So, if it is to be, I will rock him and hold him until You do. From my loving arms to Your loving arms, I surrender him to You."*

I released my hold on Davis' life and gave it to the Maker of Heaven and Earth. *This* was my hardest mom-moment. And yet, this moment of surrender gave me great peace. Peace in the midst of deep despair and fear. Peace that passes all understanding. Later that

*Our Help*

evening, Davis' fever went down. By morning it was gone. Relief and joy filled the room. I held him in my arms and thanked God for holding both of us in His.

I was isolated in the hospital room with Davis for almost two weeks. Though some of this time was tense (the days Davis had the fever were the worst), most of it was simply long and somewhat lonely. Only doctors and nurses were allowed into the room, and since Davis was still receiving strong doses of morphine, he slept off and on throughout the day. Yet there were times in the day he would be awake and alert, and I took advantage of these. A game we played daily was "Find Your Sibling." I had taped pictures of Bradley, Matthew, and Elise to Davis' crib, and when I would say a sibling's name, Davis would point to the picture. We'd celebrate his correct answers with cheers and clapping, and then we would both laugh. Simple but fun! The problem was, the game lasted maybe two minutes, and each day held a lot more minutes! I heard every tick of the clock. Occasionally, a friend or family member called to break the monotony. Wes' twin sister, Wendy, called during this time to encourage me. Even though she lived far away, she was there for us, and she was praying. Other times, I got mail. Aunt Barbara and Uncle Frank were wonderful about keeping in touch and reminding me how much they and their church were praying for everyone in our family. They were

*Consolation*

faithful, loving prayer warriors. Calls and notes like these helped the minutes pass more quickly, but most of the time, the days moved slowly for my buddy Davis and me.

Davis usually took long naps in the afternoon. This was my opportunity to leave the room while the nurses kept a close watch on him. After he fell asleep, I would pick up a pager from the nurses' station and then go to a little deli in the hospital. I got a grilled ham and cheese sandwich with tomato slices and a soda every day. Then I slowly walked back to Davis' room. On the way, I passed through a long hallway with windows on both sides. On sunny days I would sit in this hallway, turn my face to the sun, close my eyes, and pretend I was on a beach somewhere far away. Even though it was January in Wisconsin, the hallway was wonderfully warm with the afternoon sunlight pouring in. This was my quiet escape—and though it was simple and probably not worth noting, I looked forward to it day after day. One night, after Davis fell asleep, the nurses encouraged me to get out of the hospital. *We'll watch Davis*, they promised, so I went to a nearby mall. I had one hour to walk around. I even purchased a sweatshirt. When I returned to the floor carrying a shopping bag, the nurses cheered. They called it "retail-therapy" and were happy to see I had attended my first session. Transplant nurses are the best!

*Our Help*

After two weeks, Wes came back to Milwaukee. I was glad for him to see how well Davis was doing. Davis' blood counts were increasing every day. He now had energy to play with his toys and watch a short movie about a purple dinosaur named Barney. Visitors were allowed back in the room providing they scrubbed up to their elbows for five minutes (a small sink was just outside our door) and wore a mask and gown. Davis loved seeing Nana and PaPa again, and their company was such a blessing to me after the isolation of the past few weeks. I appreciated their willingness to come; it must have been very hard for them to see their little grandbaby so sick. Dave and Jean also came up to visit, giving Wes and me an opportunity to go out and get a quick bite to eat. It was our first time together, just the two of us, since Davis' diagnosis. Jean also offered to stay with Davis overnight, allowing Wes and me to stay at hotel Ronald McDonald. Jean was willing to give up a good night's sleep so I could have one—how very thoughtful.

The next morning, Wes went back to the hospital to care for Davis, and I drove home. I was anxious to see Matthew so I could gauge how he was doing with his treatment. When both Wes and I were in Milwaukee, we relied on our amazing friends and family to take Matthew to his appointments, chemotherapy, and special tests. But it was time for me to see him with my own eyes. When I got home, I was pleased to see Matthew doing well, very well. His activity level was up and his skin color looked healthy. I was encouraged to see him playing soccer in the basement with Bradley. Elise cuddled with me while I watched the boys' game. I was enjoying every minute of this and hoped to stay home for the full week as we'd planned, but I knew we would have to take it a day at a time.

I'd been home two days. Wes called. I could hear panic in his voice—again. Was it another cold or fever? No, this time it was great news: Davis' counts were high enough to make the big move from the HOT unit in the hospital to the Ronald McDonald House across the street! He could be transported the very next day. Wes was grateful but also very nervous. It was going to be a lot of work to move everything *and* learn how to care for Davis' needs in less than 24 hours. We were both afraid we couldn't offer Davis the same critical care he received at the hospital. Going from an intensive care unit to the Ronald McDonald house was a big leap, but Davis was ready to meet the outside world again—well, at least two other environments, the Ronald McDonald House and the pediatric oncology clinic. The next day, miraculously, Wes was able to move everything over to the RMH, including Davis. After they were settled, the home health nurse arrived and covered all the instructions for Davis' medicine and for the portable IV

*Our Help*

pump Davis would need for weeks to come. There was a great deal to learn, but Wes quickly got the hang of it. We were officially off the HOT unit floor!

A few days later, my sister, Ruth, flew from her home in New York to Chicago for a visit. I was so thankful; I really missed her, and I knew she was worried about us. It was the perfect time because we had a special event planned. It was "Wetherell Family Weekend" at the Ronald McDonald House. Ruth and I, along with Bradley, Matthew, and Elise, took a road trip to see Wes and Davis. We were all together again, plus Aunt Ruth—what a bonus! Every minute was cherished. Ruth's fun, upbeat personality provided a lot of laughter for our whole family. My kids loved silly Aunt Ruth, but I also appreciated my sister's loving, sympathetic care for me that weekend. Her presence lifted my spirits after the long, stressful weeks in the hospital.

But all good things must come to an end, and on Sunday afternoon, Wes, Ruth, and the three kids had to make their trek back to Glen Ellyn. Ruth had to catch a flight home, and Wes needed to go to work in the morning. It was my turn to stay with Davis for the week. When Wes asked the kids to get in the car, the tears began to stream down their cheeks. Bradley started to cry first; then Matthew joined in. Since they were crying, Elise did, too, and Ruth and I had tears in our eyes as we hugged each other goodbye. They drove away, and Davis and I headed back into the Ronald McDonald House. It was just the two of us again. That night, I felt sad, lonely, and tired. I had been strong for so long, but now I simply wanted to go home. I didn't want to worry about cancer and when it would all end—and how. Oh, the weight of how it might end haunted me. Too many "what-ifs" filled my mind.

I wasn't alone in this. I was surrounded by other families struggling with similar emotions. At the RMH, Wes and I met three such families. Each one had a boy with leukemia. Like Davis, each boy was recovering from a bone marrow transplant. The first was the Dewan family. Their baby boy, Matthew, had been diagnosed with leukemia at five months. He was less than a year old when he had his transplant. Baby Matthew was super cute, and his parents were friendly and kind. I felt an immediate connection with Matthew's mom, Fran. The Dewans had four other young kids at home in Oak Lawn. Unfortunately, none of the siblings was a match, so they used an unrelated donor for the transplant. They, too, were hoping to go home soon. I loved holding baby Matthew; he was just a few months younger than Davis and still in the snuggle stage. I could have held him for hours!

Brian Jones was an eight-year-old boy struggling with post-transplant complications. His dad, Jeff, and stepmom, Dianah, had been at CHW for over

*Our Help*

five months when we met. They were from Arkansas, so very far from family and friends. Since Brian did not have any matched siblings, Jeff ended up being his donor. He was not a perfect match, but it was their only option. CHW was one of the best transplant hospitals in the country for unrelated donors, and families came to CHW from all over, hoping for a miracle. This was the case for the Jones family. Brian had had his transplant in the fall but remained at CHW because he struggled with graft vs. host disease. All the meds pumped into this young boy completely disfigured his face, skin, and body. Dianah showed me a picture of him in second grade, taken months before he was diagnosed. The boy in the picture didn't look anything like the Brian I knew. Sadly, he felt even worse. It was a good moment when we could get him to crack a smile. My heart ached for this boy. How could something so awful happen to children like Brian? It made my stomach turn and added another dimension of concern for my own boys. Worry was my constant enemy.

Austin's family was from the East Coast. This lively six-year-old had the dreaded Philadelphia chromosome marker. His prognosis, like Davis', was in the "very poor" category. Austin, though, won my heart quickly. He was expressive, upbeat, super sweet, and a ball of energy—a delightful boy, despite all he had been through that year. Everyone loved hanging out with Austin.

*Consolation*

Four families, with four boys with leukemia, with four transplants—all living at the RMH. We spent time together, sharing and comparing stories. Our friendship grew quickly. We ate meals together, visited the Milwaukee Zoo, had a pizza party at the RMH—and cried together when our children weren't looking. We were all in the waiting stage of this nightmare, and we wondered which one would make it, and which one would not. We understood the reality of this deadly disease, and we experienced it all too soon. Matthew Dewan and Austin died in the spring, and dear Brian died a year later.

Wes and I attended baby Matthew's funeral. There's nothing sadder than looking at a baby casket. My heart broke for Fran and her family. The following year Fran and I went to Brian's funeral in Arkansas. Dianah, Fran, and I had a special bond. I loved these incredible, heartbroken moms. I wept for them and their immense loss, and they wept for me. They both said the dread of death is almost as debilitating and terrifying as death itself, but as we hugged each other goodbye, I knew they would give anything to be in my shoes.

Dianah told me she went home and flushed every pill down the toilet right after Brian died. She didn't want any more reminders of how sick he had become with graft vs. host disease. What a long fight he endured. Well, no more—Brian was free. Austin, Brian, baby Matthew—I look forward to seeing you in heaven someday.

## Chapter 14

# Your Faithfulness

*But this I call to mind and therefore I have hope:*
*The steadfast love of the Lord never ceases;*
*his mercies never come to an end;*
*they are new every morning;*
*great is your faithfulness.*
**Lamentations 3:21-23**

I appreciated being in community with these incredible families at the Ronald McDonald House, but I longed to be home. On the Monday morning after our Wetherell Family Weekend, Davis and I rode the shuttle bus to the clinic. I was thinking about the great time we'd had, all together, with my sister Ruth, but I also remembered a conversation I'd had with Bradley about his first grade open house. The open house was on Tuesday evening—the next day—and he was hoping I would be there. I had gently reminded him I couldn't

*Our Help*

go because I was in Milwaukee with Davis for the week. I assured him Dad and Grandma would be there, but the news of my absence was a deep disappointment to Bradley. I leaned my head against the bus window and closed my eyes, but I could still see his sad face. I didn't want to let him down again. An impossible hope came to my mind. *Oh, how I wish I could go*, I thought. *There must be a way.*

I decided to ask Dr. Casper if Davis and I could go home the next day. I was 99% sure he would say no, but I would try anyway, for Bradley's sake. When I asked, I talked on and on, not giving Dr. Casper a chance to say no. I shared how hard the separation had been on Bradley, and, to sway him with a medical reason, I reminded him I had another child with leukemia who also needed his mom home. "Dr. Casper, if it doesn't in any way put Davis at risk, can we please go home for one day, please?" I couldn't look at him; I didn't want to see his rejection. Dr. Casper was a strict, conservative doctor who worried deeply about his patients and never, ever took a chance with their recovery and survival. We were grateful for his no-nonsense, protective approach, so I braced myself for his negative response.

"Yes, you two can go." Yes? YES! Dr. Casper not only gave us the thumbs-up to leave the hospital campus for a day but also gave us permission to stay home one night—providing we were in his office the following morning at

*Your Faithfulness*

nine o'clock sharp. Deal! I called Wes and told him the good news but asked him not to tell Bradley. I wanted it to be a surprise. The next day, after getting instructions from our home health nurse on how to transport Davis with his IV pump and after arranging detailed home health care while home for the night—how I got this done on such short notice, I will never know—we were on our way. I thanked God every mile I was further away from the hospital and closer to my home.

Two hours later, we arrived. Perfect timing: school had just ended and Bradley was starting his walk home. I anxiously looked down the sidewalk from our driveway, waiting for Bradley to turn onto our street. There he was! The sight of him walking along, chatting with a neighbor friend, unaware of my presence, thrilled me. Then he spotted me. Immediately his face lit up, and he yelled, "Mom!" He ran toward me, smiling from ear to ear, yelling as he got closer. "Mom! You're home! You came home!" He jumped into my arms, and I swung him around, hugging him tight. Then I set him down, looked him right in the eyes, and said, "Bradley, I came home just for you. I can't wait to go to your Open House tonight."

Redemption. Bradley guided me around his school that night, pointing out his desk, his art projects, the gym, everything. It was his night. I took it all in, catching up on what I had missed and learning something wonderful about Bradley's character in the process. Even though

*Our Help*

home life was rough, not only did he persevere at school, he thrived. Bradley happily introduced me to his teacher and many new friends. I saw an excitement and joy on his face I hadn't seen in a while, but the best thing I saw that night was how God cared for my son when I couldn't. Thankfully, that night, I *was* with him. And it was sweet.

Dr. Casper was impressed with how well we did at home (and, yes, I was back at the clinic at nine a.m. sharp the next morning) and told us we could make preparations to move back home at the end of the week! We couldn't believe it! Davis would still need to see Dr. Casper three times a week in clinic, but we could go home. Wes came up on Friday to help me pack; we said our tearful goodbyes to the other wonderful families at the Ronald McDonald House; and the three of us drove back to Glen Ellyn together. What a blessing—and what perfect timing. I was growing more concerned about my other little guy fighting cancer. Matthew was two weeks away from the most difficult phase of his chemo regimen, and he would definitely need both Mom and Dad by his side.

Delayed Intensification is a really nasty phase in the chemotherapy process. The nurses warned us Matthew might need to be hospitalized during this phase. The chemo was much stronger and more aggressive, significantly weakening his immune system in the process.

*Your Faithfulness*

These strong doses would also remove any strands of hair still on his little head. Sure enough, after two rounds of chemo, Matthew went completely bald. It happened so suddenly it was quite shocking. He went to bed with hair and woke up with none. That morning, I walked into Bradley and Matthew's room to wake them up and sat down on the edge of Matthew's bed. All the hair that had been attached to Matthew's head when he went to bed was now scattered over his pillow. I gasped but then caught myself so as not to scare Matthew. I quickly said, "Guess what, Matthew? You're not going to believe this, but last night something amazing happened. You look like Michael Jordan. Go run and see." He ran as fast as his wobbly legs could down the hall to our little bathroom. He jumped up on the toilet seat and leaned over to take a good look in the mirror. He ran his hand over his shiny, hairless head—sure enough, just like MJ! He thought his new look was super cool.

Unfortunately, the "cool" factor faded once the effects of the chemo kicked in. Soon Matthew felt extremely lethargic, occasionally irritable, and just plain "out-of-it." He slept, watched TV, and, at times, if his energy level was up, played for a few minutes with his siblings. Bradley and Elise were great buddies for him since he could not have any friends over. Miraculously, Matthew didn't get a fever or a virus during those tough weeks, so he never had to be hospitalized. His skin coloring was

*Our Help*

dull and yellow, and his emotions were at times extreme, but his tough-guy spirit gave him the strength to endure much more than I could have at his age. I was so grateful to be with him and not up in Milwaukee. He felt so sick and weak, but this time I was there to care for him; I was able to hold him and give him the comfort only a mom can. I thanked God over and over for His gracious and perfect timing. I knew it could have been much worse for all of us. God's powerful protection for Matthew not only greatly benefited him but also helped his brother Davis. Since Matthew wasn't hospitalized, we were able to keep up with the constant trips to Milwaukee.

Dr. Casper was still very concerned for Davis. Three months had passed since the transplant, and we were fast approaching Davis' next big hurdle: the 100-day-post-transplant visit in Milwaukee. During this visit, Davis would have a bone marrow aspiration and a spinal. Dr. Casper reminded us of the seriousness of these test results and the grim realities of Davis' leukemia. If even the smallest trace of leukemic cells were found in his marrow, Davis would most likely relapse with no other options available. He had reached his life's quota of chemo. He would not be given any more if he relapsed. The fight would be over.

Living with this potential death sentence was almost unbearable. We were hopeful but aware that terrible news was a very real possibility. Baby Matthew Dewan

*Your Faithfulness*

had his 100-day visit the week before ours. Dr. Casper checked his bone marrow right after the procedure and found leukemic cells. There were no follow-up tests, no discussions of further treatment. Nothing else could be done for Baby Matthew. Fran called me that very night with the horrible news. I was shocked at the finality of it.

Now it was our turn to head up to Milwaukee.

When we arrived at the clinic, they called us to a procedure room and immediately sedated Davis. Wes and I watched as Dr. Casper began the aspiration. He drew enough marrow to smear a small amount on nine slides. He placed these, one by one, on a sterile tray. I silently prayed over each one of those slides, asking God for healthy, cancer-free marrow. Beside me, Wes was doing the same. Before the slides were sent to the lab, Dr. Casper put the ninth slide under his microscope. He asked us to wait in a small, cold room nearby while he examined it. This was the same room the Dewans had been in a week before. I felt sick, thinking of the Dewans, then of Davis. Baby Matthew, then *my* baby. My mind circled round and round; my gut clenched tight. Finally we saw Dr. Casper step into the hallway. Wes said, "Here he comes." I couldn't look, couldn't breathe. I stared at Wes' face. I *wanted* to hear Dr. Casper's words—and I didn't want to. He spoke as he entered the room. "I don't see any leukemia. It looks good for now." Big

*Our Help*

exhale. My blood started flowing. My stomach relaxed. We had been given more time with Davis. *Time is a gift.* Dr. Casper warned us Davis could still relapse; there was just no sign of that happening at present. We understood, but this day, we were celebrating. *Today is a gift.* All the way home we called family and friends who'd been faithfully praying. We passed the 100-day test!

We moved into our new house that spring. It wouldn't have happened without the help of many, many people. Since clinic days continued to fill up a good portion of my days and weeks, Tara had to box up almost the entire house, while also taking care of Elise and Bradley. What a blessing she was to me. She packed it all up—and on move-in day, a team of family and friends unpacked it. I was amazed how quickly the rooms came together; we all slept comfortably, in beds, the very first night. Shortly after we moved, Matthew began his maintenance phase of treatment, which meant less intense chemo and fewer visits to the clinic. After eight months, we were finally home more days during the week than at the clinic or hospital. Incredible.

When my clinic schedule changed, so did my dependence on Tara. She'd been with us eight months, but her job was coming to an end. Tara's weekly salary was paid through a trust fund set up by our church. Oh, how God was in the details: He supplied not only Tara but also the means by which to hire and keep

*Your Faithfulness*

her. She was sent to us by God—I told her this many times. She invested her heart and soul into our kids. She loved and took good care of them while I was away. When our home life was in turmoil, her gentle, consistent spirit made it a safe place for my children. She made delicious dinners, tackled the wash, and kept the house just the way I liked it. I never once felt stressed about household duties; she took care of them all. It was hard to see her go, but we both knew it was time. My kids were doing well, and I was able to focus on everyone in my family and manage our home life again. On her last day, we hugged each other good-bye and cried happy tears. I won't ever forget her. Thank you, Tara.

Life was moving forward. The spring and summer brought renewed hope. Bradley played park district soccer and finished up a great year at Ben Franklin. Elise blossomed from toddler to little girl overnight. One of the many things I loved about this little girl stage was her laugh. She would crinkle up her freckled nose and give me the cutest giggle. Matthew and Davis' hair was growing back—what a great sign we were on the road to recovery! We called Matthew's hair "angel hair" because it grew back wonderfully soft, curly, and golden (he had dark hair before). *Everyone* wanted to touch it. Davis finally started gaining weight, and his skin coloring improved. Both boys had those awful central lines

*Our Help*

removed, and shortly after, Matthew had a port-a-cath surgically placed under his skin for future chemo injections during the maintenance phase. He was thrilled the port site could get wet; this meant he could swim (he couldn't do that with a central line). On our first day back to the pool, he went right over to his favorite jumping spot from the year before. "Wow, what a year he's had," I thought as I watched him, "and yet here he is again, jumping in the pool like a super hero."

With life stabilizing, I began to exhale, but this "letting-down" process came with its own challenges. The anxiety attacks returned, and I realized I was dealing with post-traumatic stress. I had a tightness in my throat and a sadness that wouldn't let up. At night, I would wake up in a sweat, worried something was terribly wrong. I would slip out of bed and check on all four children, just to make sure. I lived in the "what-if" stage for a very long time. I knew too much. I was terrified to go back to the dark side of more chemo, more bad news, no more options. Wes and I worried and wondered over every blood test, every bone marrow aspiration, and every spinal test. Living with the threat of relapse was a daily emotional challenge, but God continued to comfort and calm our hearts and minds. He reminded us over and over He was in control, and over time we found ourselves enjoying the present rather than worrying about the future.

*Your Faithfulness*

Matthew continued with two more years of chemotherapy on a monthly basis. Our trips to see Dr. Hayani were manageable, and the kids, even Bradley and Elise, enjoyed visiting their favorite doctor. Dr. Hayani was amazed at how tough Matthew was when it came to bone marrow aspirations and spinal taps. Most of his patients, even the older teens, asked to be sedated before these procedures. Not our Matthew. He would curl up in a ball and look right into his daddy's eyes. Wes would call out math problems, and Matthew would solve them. With all the determination he could muster, Matthew remained completely still until Dr. Hayani was finished. Afterwards he would fall asleep for thirty minutes, completely exhausted from battling his fears. But he did it! This courage for such a small boy was almost unbelievable.

One night, after a long day of chemo, I knelt by Matthew's bedside. I could tell he was weary and needed me to linger a few minutes before he fell asleep. I wanted him to feel safe when I left the room, so I told him about God's angels, how even though he couldn't see them, they were close by, watching and caring for him when he was alone, protecting him. Matthew didn't have to process this information. He didn't even ask any questions. He simply said, "I know."

I was surprised. "You do?" I asked.

Matthew sat straight up then and pointed to the end of his bed. "He sits right there, Mommy."

*Our Help*

"But how do you know, Matthew?" I was the one learning now.

"Well," he said, "when you leave the room, I feel him sit on my bed. The bed dips down when he sits down, and that's how I know he's there."

With tears in my eyes, I gave Matthew a kiss on his forehead. As I walked out of the room, I couldn't help but look back at the edge of his bed, smiling at the angel who had just started his watch.

During Matthew's maintenance phase, Davis continued to have checkups, and month after month the blood tests, the marrow checks, and the spinal taps all came back normal. Matthew's chemotherapy ended a little over three years after diagnosis, and in August of 2000, he finished his last scheduled oncology visit with Dr. Hayani. Both boys would return for annual checkups, but they had no more bone marrow aspirations, no more spinals, no more chemo, no more injections, no more pills to swallow, and no more hair loss. They were done. Davis was 6; Matthew was 10. We marked this milestone by taking a picture of Dr. Hayani with his arms around the two boys. Afterwards, our whole family went out to Pizza Hut to celebrate. Pizza never tasted so good.

And the best news ever? Dr. Hayani believed both boys were cured. Cured. Cured. I can't say or write that word enough.

CURED.

## Chapter 15

# His Way

*This God - his way is perfect,*
*the word of the* Lord *proves true;*
*he is a shield for all those who take refuge in him.*
Psalm 18:30

I am typing this chapter on a warm, sunny day in September of 2014, twenty years after Davis' and Matt's diagnoses. Not a single day has gone by in all these years without my remembering our leukemia crisis, sometimes for a brief second, other times for much longer. The story permeates my heart and mind, for through it, I experienced God's goodness and grace in a very special way, in a way that might only be possible during times of deep suffering. It's not that we've had a perfect life since leukemia, not at all; life is still life. We've had our share of different disappointments and difficulties over the past twenty years—but thankfully, we have not had leukemia.

*Our Help*

Remember the dream house I wished for, with the beautiful view out back? I've looked out my kitchen window over the years and have witnessed, again and again, God's abundant blessings on display: Bradley, Matthew, Elise, and Davis swinging on swings, chasing our new puppy, Annie, and Elise's cat, Cookie, bouncing on the trampoline, running relay races at end-of-the-year school parties, playing tag and baseball, lighting firecrackers, throwing water balloons, enjoying cookouts and many, many family reunions. I'm beyond grateful for the incredible ways God has cared for each of my children all these years. He promised to help, and He did, exceedingly, with a faithfulness that is evident even now. Brad, Matt, Elise, and Davis have grown into amazing young adults, and I am grateful for each one of them.

Brad is now working at a wonderful church as its Student Ministry Pastor. Along with investing in the lives of students and leading mission trips, Brad has the opportunity to preach. What a thrill it is to sit in church and listen to him speak God's truth to the congregation—to teach God's truth to me. It brings back wonderful memories of my dad. He, too, was a pastor. Brad is working on a degree at Trinity Evangelical Divinity School and will graduate next spring. Before Trinity, he attended Taylor University and was on the track team all four years. His favorite race was the 4x400 relay.

*His Way*

Brad doesn't talk much about our leukemia days, but I know he has a better perspective now that he's an adult. I have a clearer perspective, too. I see how God used our leukemia crisis for Brad's good. God was shaping Brad's sensitive and tender heart long before Brad knew God was calling him into the ministry. Brad is uniquely qualified to offer a message of help and hope to those who feel abandoned or forgotten, to those who struggle with disappointing loss. God redeemed his crushed spirit and filled his childhood and teen years with many great experiences and memories. Brad is a kind and thoughtful man who cares deeply for people. He's a loyal friend; people trust him. He still loves to learn and grow—rarely do you find him without a good book close by. I praise God for how He has provided and cared for Brad. God's most recent gift to him is his beautiful bride, Kristen, a kind, talented woman who is a wonderful complement to our family. They married this past May. The wedding was one of the happiest days of our family's life. Wes and I love Brad and Kristen so very much.

Matt works at a recruiting firm in the Chicagoland area. He went to college in Minnesota, at Bethel University, where he was the place kicker for the football team all four years and a rugby player his junior and senior years. Yes, he's quite competitive—the harder the hit, the better. Matt has a winsome, energetic, and determined spirit. He's a happy guy who brings joy to others.

*Our Help*

He reminds us all of Papa Wetherell, both in personality and definitely in appearance. He's relational and sensitive to the emotions of others. God has gifted Matt with empathy so he can care for others, comforting them with the same comfort he's received from God. Matt has reached out to many people burdened by cancer, especially leukemia, telling them his story, encouraging them, and giving them visible hope.

Except for two serious bouts of pneumonia and a nasty case of shingles, Matt was fairly healthy and strong during his maintenance phase of chemotherapy. But, five to eight years *after* diagnosis, Matt showed frustration with reading, and he had trouble concentrating in class and finishing school assignments. Reading processing delays and ADHD are very common "late effects" among children who received high doses of the drug methotrexate at a young age. But these challenges didn't stop Matt; he persevered and graduated from Bethel with a bachelor of science degree in communications. God has been abundantly faithful and gracious to Matt. He protected him over and over throughout his growing-up years, and we are thankful, so very thankful, Matt never relapsed. Wes and I love Matt so very much.

Elise just started a masters program at Taylor University after graduating from Bethel University this past spring with a degree in environmental studies. God provided her with many wonderful experiences at

*His Way*

Bethel, especially as a Residence Assistant during her junior and senior years. Elise has a courageous and independent spirit, as evidenced by her decision to spend her sophomore year studying in New Zealand. It was a spectacular place for Elise to witness God's handiwork in creation. God has given Elise a passion to honor Him and help others by caring for all that He's created.

Elise has grown to love the simple and more important things in life, such as deep friendships, family traditions, and meaningful conversations over a good cup of coffee. She is a great encourager and easily communicates her love and appreciation in special ways. She has benefited from being the only girl in a family with three boys: she's petite and feminine, yet also strong and confident—and all this is wrapped up in one beautiful young lady. Her outlook on life is filled with hope—a wonderful irony we love and appreciate. Elise has seen over and over how God has beautifully, lovingly provided for her. Wes and I love Elise so very much.

Growing up, Elise and Davis enjoyed a special bond. They spent countless hours hanging out together, playing and talking. Maybe this special connection is because they're only twenty-one months apart in age; maybe it's because they are the two youngest in our family; or maybe it's because Davis and Elise now share the same DNA since transplant. I think it's all of the above. Elise has been known to wittingly play the "I saved your life"

*Our Help*

card when she wants Davis to do something for her, and Davis likes to compliment Elise with these affectionate words: "I, literally, wouldn't be able to live without her." Well said. They continue to enjoy a close relationship and are now able to spend a lot of time together, since Elise is attending the same university as Davis and living only a block away from him. If all goes according to plan, the two of them will graduate on the same day in the same ceremony. What a journey they've had together.

Davis is a junior at Taylor University pursuing a degree in English with a concentration in literature. He oversees all the discipleship assistants in his dorm and is involved with Student Senate. He loves to interact with just about anyone at Taylor, peer or professor. Davis is a great conversationalist and a wonderful listener. He loves to read and write and he's very good at both. He, like Brad, has an ever-growing collection of books.

I really wish I could say life has been perfect for Davis after surviving cancer, but healing has come at a cost. Over the years, Davis' body has suffered the results of that hard and difficult fight at such a young age, and his battle wounds continue to show up as the years go by. Davis has had cataract surgery in both eyes. In third grade, he had hip surgery to fix a slipped hip. Because of his weakened hip, the orthopaedic doctor told him he could not run or jump for six to eight years. It was heartbreaking news, especially after getting a trampoline

*His Way*

for his Make-A-Wish. (We were grateful when, after two years, that idea was dismissed.) Davis had a melanoma scare that left him with his biggest surgical scar—straight across the center of his chest. He had a benign growth removed from his shoulder. Davis endured seven years of daily growth hormone shots that proved unsuccessful in assisting him to reach a height of 5 feet. As a junior in high school, he had his toughest year when the doctor attempted to correct and straighten his legs through two osteotomy surgeries, three months apart. After six tough, painful months, the left was corrected and the right was not. Our entire family felt disappointed and discouraged following this result. Matt, especially, hurt for Davis. It was really hard for him to watch Davis suffer more with leukemia than he did. We all think Davis has endured enough.

All of Davis' physical problems are a result of the radiation and strong chemotherapy he had as a baby. But God has been unbelievably good to Davis. These challenges have highlighted Davis' inner strength. Every time he's been knocked down, he's rebounded even stronger. The medical side effects, no matter how serious they were, never set Davis back, not mentally, not emotionally, and not spiritually. This resilience has had an impact on the lives of others. When people hang around Davis, they are encouraged and strengthened. People look up to Davis. He is a brilliant thinker and a natural leader who uses both these gifts to speak boldly about his faith in Jesus. Davis loves his life—what a powerful witness to God's faithfulness. We thank God for Davis' joyful spirit throughout his childhood. We thank God he never relapsed. And yes, Wes and I love Davis so very much.

## Chapter 16

# The Best Help

*O God, from my youth you have taught me;
and I still proclaim your wondrous deeds. So
even to old age and gray hairs, O God do not
forsake me, until I proclaim your might to another
generation, your power to all those to come.*
**Psalm 71: 17-18**

*For you have been my help,
and in the shadow of your wings I will sing for joy.*
**Psalm 63:7**

This is my story about leukemia. This is my story about my family and leukemia. More importantly, this is my story about God as my promised Help, our promised Help. I have written this story for my four dear children, their spouses, and my future grandbabies. My

*Our Help*

hope is that they will experience and trust God's help when they encounter their own trials along life's way. And in the following and final pages, I would like to share one more amazing lesson: an insight into deeper matters. Over the years, I've learned how our leukemia story reminds me of a far greater, far better story, one Wes and I told our children all through their childhood. It is God's Story and it's written all through the pages of the Holy Bible. God wrote it long ago, yet its message is for everyone. It's a message about the best help ever.

All of us, at some point in life, experience pain, brokenness, helplessness. We create much of this pain and brokenness ourselves. We are born with the ability to hurt others, hurt ourselves, deceive others, and deceive ourselves. We fight, rebel, blame, lie, hate. We make a mess of our lives through selfish behaviors, addictive patterns, and unwise decisions. Even when we're living a "good, moral life" and making good decisions, tragedy can strike. We get sick; loved ones get sick; children get cancer. We lose jobs; we lose friends. Marriages break down and families separate. We have accidents and encounter a multitude of unpredicted challenges. The list goes on and on. If we are blessed with a long life, we grow old. We die. Life *is* beautiful, but eventually we will all experience something that will cause us to say, "Life is unfair. Life is broken. I'm broken." Thankfully, God knows and understands. He has a plan to rescue us

*The Best Help*

from this troubled, broken world and to save us from our sinful nature.

Sin is our cancer, the cancer we all have. Sin is rebellion against the living God and His will for us. We have it from birth, and it's terminal. Some people don't know they have this disease, but they do. Some haven't yet experienced its symptoms, but they will. Some believe their "disease" (sin) is not as bad as God, our great Physician, says it is, but it is. We reject God's warnings and diagnosis, and we rebel against His truthful examination of our hearts. The Bible tells us that our hearts are deceitful and desperately sick.

Can you imagine what would have happened if Wes and I had denied the serious truth that Davis and Matthew had leukemia? What if we had become angry with Dr. Hayani for delivering such awful news? What if we'd said, "We've never seen any leukemic cells, so how could it be true?" How absurd and foolish. Yet that's how many of us live today in regard to our sin and its consequences. We don't want to hear the news. But the truth still remains; we are sinners and we are in grave danger. Sin doesn't just make our lives hard—the equivalent of the initial pain or fatigue caused by cancer; sin alienates us from God, our true source of life. "For the wages of sin is death..." (Romans 6:23). Sin is why we all experience death, both physically and spiritually. Prognosis: dismal. We need help. We need a cure.

*Our Help*

We try so many ways to "cure" this disease ourselves, but God has the only effective treatment plan. Actually, His plan is more than "effective." It is the perfect, miraculous protocol that heals us completely. His plan has a name: Jesus Christ, God's only Son. God, who is holy and righteous, sent Jesus to earth to be our Savior. He lived a perfect, sinless life. When He grew up, he proclaimed, "I am the way, and the truth and the life. No one comes to the Father except through me"(John 14:6). People hated Jesus for making himself equal with God, so one dark day, they beat him, placed a crown of thorns on His head and nailed Him to a cross to die. And yet, this was God's plan all along. Hundreds of years before Jesus' birth, Isaiah prophesied Jesus' death. "He was pierced for our transgressions; he was crushed for our iniquities; upon him was the chastisement that brought us peace, and with his wounds we are healed. All we like sheep have gone astray; we have turned—everyone—to his own way; and the Lord has laid on him the iniquity of us all" (Isaiah 53:5-6). The Bible also says, "For our sake he (God the Father) made him (God the Son) to be sin who knew no sin, so that we might become the righteousness of God" (2 Corinthians 5:21).

Jesus took the punishment for our sin. He experienced God's wrath toward our sin. He experienced separation from His Fatther. He sacrificed His perfect life for sinners. He willingly went to the cross and paid the

*The Best Help*

penalty for our sin. He did this because He loves us! "While we were still sinners (forever helpless), Christ died for us" (Romans 5:8).

And the news gets better. Jesus did not stay dead. He rose from the grave breaking the power of sin and death. Many peope witnessed his resurrection before he ascended back to heaven. Jesus is alive. He is the Savior of the world, the Promised One and He offers salvation and eternal life to all people everywhere. This is the Gospel and this is very good news for our very sick souls. "The wages of sin is death but the gift of God is eternal life through Jesus Christ our Lord" (Romans 6:23).

When we begin to see the seriousness of our sin diagnosis, God doesn't leave us in despair. He extends amazing grace and says, "I will help you." He calls us to repent (to admit and grieve our sin because we know it offends a Holy God). He calls us to believe, and God gives us the gift of faith to trust and believe His Son's sacrificial work on the cross. He mercifully forgives our sins—*oh the healing power of forgiveness*! He gives His Spirit to live within us. We now have the power to change, to turn from our selfish and sinful ways, and to love and obey the true and living God. When we submit to His call, we see life differently. We view it with a confident hope because we know God keeps His promises, and He promises to never leave us or forsake us, no matter what circumstances we face in life here on earth. We also have hope because we have life beyond this earth, eternal life—one day we will meet Christ face to face. One day, we will finally be home. "He will wipe away every tear from their eyes, and death shall be no more, neither shall there be mourning, nor crying, nor pain anymore, for the former things have passed away" (Revelation 21:4).

Before the transplant, Davis' marrow was full of deadly cancer. His marrow produced leukemic cells that would eventually kill him if left untreated. His marrow needed to be destroyed and replaced with new, life-sustaining marrow. What a beautiful picture of biblical salvation. From the minute we are born, sin-filled blood runs through us all, leading eventually to death and separation from God (hell). But through the work of salvation, through faith in Jesus Christ, God wondrously transforms us. He replaces the old with new. Our spiritual DNA changes—and, over time, we become more Christ-like. We are children of God and physical death is now a door to heaven, to eternal life with our Heavenly Father. Jesus calls this process being "born again," and the Apostle Paul describes this rebirth as a new creation. "Therefore, if anyone is in Christ, he is a new creation. The old has passed away; behold, the new has come" (2 Corinthians 5:17).

Only through Jesus can we be rescued, renewed and restored. Forever cured. **Our help is in the name of the**

**Lord, and that name is Jesus.** The Lord Jesus Christ is our best help.

If both Matthew and Davis had died of leukemia years ago, would I proclaim this Good News to the next generation? Or am I devoted to God *only* because He healed my two boys (although, they will still face death someday)? I have had to ask myself those questions with an honest examination of my heart and my motives. Here's my answer: I love, glorify, and give my life to God because He is God. He's my Savior. I trust Him even when He leads me "through the valley of the shadow of death." My circumstances or my feelings about Him do not define Him. His Word does. His Son Jesus does. He does. I did not write my story primarily because Davis and Matthew lived. I wrote this story because God lives. He's the living God who made heaven and earth. Because He lives, he hears my cry for help. Because He lives, He has the power to help. And He has promised to be my help throughout all of life and into eternity. No matter what I go through, I am His.

My faith in the Gospel was not tested by the deaths of my sons, but I've known others who have endured just such a test and have still found God to be all He promised. I have a dear friend, Terri Bradford, whose teen nephew, Matthew Anderson, passed away from leukemia a few years ago. Matthew's parents are Christians, and so was Matthew. His faith was anchored in Jesus Christ.

*Our Help*

We all prayed and prayed for Matthew to be healed, but God had different plans for this courageous young man, plans that caused sorrow for his family but ultimately joy for Matthew. He died months after his bone marrow transplant. He and Davis were on the same fantasy baseball team just weeks before he passed away. Nothing, absolutely nothing, feels right about that ending...it's so very sad.

But if you were to talk with this young man's mom and dad, they would still be a witness to our true God and could share the many ways God has been their help in the midst of much sorrow. Behind their tears are eyes filled with the certain hope that one day they will be reunited with their son. That's what God promises for those who are His own. He has a better, greater plan for His people than what this life brings, and His plan is the help we need. This is why so many Christians can say with confidence, "It is well with my soul," no matter what trial or circumstance they face. They know the bottom line: God can be trusted. He can be trusted with our daily struggles as well as our future glory beyond this life. The old familiar hymn states this truth well, "Strength for today and bright hope for tomorrow. Great is Thy faithfulness."

I am amazed at God. His steadfast love, goodness, and grace will always overwhelm me. All through my life, He has been faithful and so very, very good to me. On a long-ago September day, He promised His powerful help to me and to my family as we headed into danger and despair. Through lesson after lesson He taught me to trust this promise. He helped Wes, Brad, Matt, Elise, and Davis. He helped me.

Above all, I thank God for our greatest and best help, Jesus Christ. I rejoice in knowing, "all the promises of God find their Yes in him. That is why it is through him that we utter our Amen to God for his glory" (2 Corinthians 1:20).

Jesus is our Help - what a magnificent promise.

# Afterword

*... And we know that for those who love God all things work together for good, for those who are called according to his purpose.*
**Romans 8:28**

Beth and I both grew up in wonderful Christian homes, and verses like the one above were very familiar to us. Real life, though, tests our understanding of these truths and requires us to ask, "What do I really believe?"—especially when life isn't what we had hoped for.

As Beth has shared here, this chapter of our life put the truth of this promise to the test. Experientially, we realized—in a way we could not have otherwise understood—this promise is actually true.

*"**All things** work together for good..."* It has been easy for Beth and me to see good in much of life, but we had never faced a problem of this magnitude. I was numb, angry, and crushed, all at the same time. No one wants to hear their children's futures described by a statistic! What possible good comes from sickness and suffering? How could this story result in anything good? I already

*Afterword*

knew this verse was true, but I needed to *experience* the truth of it as well.

Beth's story describes how we experienced this in many very unexpected places. We found we were part of a bigger story than our own. We realized more deeply that we are not the focus of life's story, and we found meaning and comfort in recognizing that what mattered most was not our purposes, but that we had been "*called according to **his** purpose.*"

I found God especially used my weaknesses to point this out. In Chapter 10, Beth mentioned a Christmas party I wanted us to attend during our initial chemotherapy regime, and my being "disappointed" at having to take Davis to the hospital instead of attending. That was a kind description of my reaction. To be honest, I was a jerk. I drove Davis to the hospital that night feeling sorry for myself and mad at everyone and everything. I got to the hospital and found the room wasn't equipped appropriately. I charged out towards the nurses' station ready to give anyone there a piece of my mind. In mid stride, I was stopped when someone grabbed me by the arm. It was one of the parents we had come to know on the floor. He said he was glad to see me, and then he called to someone across the hall. There, sitting on the floor, leaning against a closed hospital door, was a man I had never met. With excitement, my friend said to him, "Here's the guy I mentioned. Here's the guy who

*Our Help*

believes in Jesus." I discovered his daughter had just been diagnosed with leukemia. I sat on the floor with him listening to his story, realizing that there was a greater purpose for me that night than merely attending a party. God had an appointment for me; and when I saw the event with God's purpose in mind, it changed what had disappointed me into something… well, good.

When I quote Romans 8:28 to my kids, I frequently ask them whether the verse says "some things" or "all things." This reminds me of what we're continuing to learn about what really matters in life. God's plan is better than mine, and trusting him makes all of life—even the difficulties—good.

But this promise is made to a specific group of people: *"…those who love God."* God revealed himself in Jesus Christ (Colossians 1:19), and we love him because of Jesus' love for us (1 John 4:9). In writing Romans 8, Paul points to this when he says:

*He who did not spare his own Son but gave him up for us all, how will he not also with him graciously give us **all things**? – Romans 8:32*

Beth and I are continuing to learn this truth experientially. We pray that this story encourages you to trust in the God who keeps His word, whose promises are true, and whose love is worth trusting, even in the darkest days of your life. After all, as Paul concludes:

*Afterword*

*"What then shall we say to these things? If God is for us, who can be against us? He who did not spare his own Son but gave him up for us all, how will he not also with him graciously give us all things? Who shall bring any charge against God's elect? It is God who justifies. Who is to condemn? Christ Jesus is the one who died—more than that, who was raised—who is at the right hand of God, who indeed is interceding for us. Who shall separate us from the love of Christ? Shall tribulation, or distress, or persecution, or famine, or nakedness, or danger, or sword? As it is written,*

> *'For your sake we are being killed all the day long; we are regarded as sheep to be slaughtered.'*

*No, in **all these things** we are more than conquerors through him who loved us. For I am sure that neither death nor life, nor angels nor rulers, nor things present nor things to come, nor powers, nor height nor depth, nor anything else in all creation, will be able to separate us from the love of God in Christ Jesus our Lord.*

– Romans 8:31-39

# Acknowledgements

Thank you Jennifer Underwood for editing my story. Your wisdom, expertise and encouragement gave me the confidence to complete an important and personal goal. I am so grateful for you.

Thank you, Dr. Hayani, for years and years of compassionate medical care. God has used your life to help ours. Thank you, Dr. Betti, Dr. Casper, and all the nurses who cared for our family.

I'm thankful for incredible friends who have supported us during and after this crisis, including our small group, Trent and Terri Bradford, George and Leslie Petro, and Ann and Rob Wyant. Thank you to my long-time dance instructor and friend, Sharon Scherr. When I'm in your studio, the stress and anxiety seem to disappear, especially when dancing next to my sweet friend, Kendra Adeszko. Thank you to Perry and Sara Mascetti and Jeff and Lora Helton. Wes and I have been tremendously blessed by your faithful, consistent friendship. Thank you, Lora and Sara, for encouraging me to journal years ago; much of the detailed material in this story came from those tear-filled pages.

Thanks to our amazing Allen/Wetherell extended family. Thank you for your love, and thank you for your prayers. I've watched many of you walk through unexpected trials and I have witnessed God's abundant faithfulness to you. Wes and I love you all.

Thank you, Mom Wetherell, for your constant love and your never-ending prayers. You are a gift to our entire family.

Thank you Brad and Kristen, Matt, Elise and Davis for the love and joy you bring to me every day. I love being your mom.

My biggest, heartfelt appreciation goes to my husband, Wes. Wes, this story is our story. We walked this tough journey together, and I am so thankful it was you by my side. Thank you for loving me so well. Thank you for loving our children so well. I love you with all my heart.

Made in the USA
Monee, IL
05 December 2021